Elijah:
Yahweh Is My God

G. Avery Lee

BROADMAN PRESS
Nashville, Tennessee

Unless otherwise indicated, all Scripture quotations are from the Revised Standard Version of the Bible; copyrighted 1946. 1952, © 1971, 1973.

Dewey Decimal Classification: 221.92
Subject Heading: ELIJAH, PROPHET
Library of Congress Catalog Card Number: 86-26915
Printed in the United States of America

Library of Congress Cataloging-in-Publication Data

Lee, G. Avery.
  Elijah, Yahweh is my God.

  1. Elijah (Biblical prophet)—Sermons. 2. Sermons,
American. 3. Baptists—Sermons. 4. Southern Baptist
Convention—Sermons. I. Title.
BS580.E4L44   1987   252'.061   86-26915
ISBN 0-8054-1539-4

This book is affectionately dedicated to the 1980 Choir of the St. Charles Avenue Baptist Church, New Orleans, Louisiana—Dr. William S. May, Minister of Music; Dr. Thomas Mitts, Organist; and to the 1984 Choir of the University Baptist Church, Hattiesburg, Mississippi—Dr. Thomas H. Porter, Minister of Music; Mr. Sammy Polk, Organist.

Contents

Introduction

Elijah, the man second only to Moses in historic Judaism, one of the most exciting personalities in the Bible, is a larger-than-life character. His life is the "stuff" of which legends are made.

This does not mean that the stories were invented, for they are historical. It is often difficult to distinguish between fact and legend. However, we probably have a truer picture of his greatness than a strictly historical, matter-of-fact presentation could have given us. Traditions begin with events and personalities. They are an interior history of the hopes and fears, the realities and aspirations, what is thought and known to be on the one hand, and in what is believed may be on the other.

A significant truth is that this larger-than-life personality was as human as we are. He struggled with the same outer and inner conflicts that confront us. In his outward world he battled with Ahab, Jezebel, Baal, and his own people. Inwardly, he had to face up to himself and know God. He had to overcome the inner demons of rejection, depression, and fear. His victories give us encouragement.

Elijah, which means "Yahweh is God," or "Yahweh is my God," appeared from nowhere and vanished as abruptly as he appeared. His story is told in episodic form in 1 Kings 17—21 and in 2 Kings 1—2. In each episode he suddenly appeared and as quickly disappeared.

To grasp the full impact of Elijah we should look at the dynasty of Omri, of whom it was written: "Omri did what was evil in the sight of the Lord, and did more evil than all who were before him" (1 Kings 16:25).

Ahab, Omri's son, and a focal person in the Elijah story, succeeded his father as king of Israel, and it was also recorded: "And Ahab the son of Omri did evil in the sight of the Lord more than all that were before him" (v. 30).

That charge is repeated in verse 33: "Ahab did more to provoke the Lord, the God of Israel, to anger than all the kings of Israel who were before him."

That evil continued in the grandson of Omri, Ahaziah, who followed Ahab:

> He did what was evil in the sight of the Lord and walked in the way of his father, and in the way of his mother... He served Baal ... and provoked the Lord, the God of Israel, to anger in every way that his father had done (22:52-53).

Into such a legacy of evil the prophet Elijah appeared with no choice but to declare the supremacy of Yahweh and the moral nature of the universe.

There is neither genealogy nor credentials for Elijah as a prophet. He is called a Tishbite from the region of Gilead. The story begins abruptly at 1 Kings 17:1 and ends with his final disappearance in 2 Kings 2:14. The major saga is found in 1 Kings 20—22, which contains eleven episodes:

1. The first meeting with Ahab and the prediction of no rain (1 Kings 17:1).
2. Fed by ravens at Cherith's brook (vv. 2-7).
3. With the widow at Zarapeth and the death and revival of her son (vv. 8-24).
4. With Obadiah (18:1-16).
5. On Mount Carmel (vv. 17-40).
6. The end of the drought (vv. 41-46).
7. The flight to Horeb (19:1-18).
8. Recruitment of Elisha (vv. 19-21).
9. Naboth's vineyard (21:1-29).
10. Judgment on Ahaziah (2 Kings 1:1-18).
11. Elijah's ascension (2:1-14).

The context of these stories is an account of the constant struggle between faith in Yahweh (God) and the other gods and cultures of the region. We see the reminder of the First Commandment: "You shall have no other gods before me" (Deut. 5:7). Elijah won the conflict, but Baalism was not wiped out; Baalism is never wiped out in this life.

This battle was theological, not political. And let's remember that we have a biased record. Both Omri and Ahab were politically astute kings. In that respect, they were probably the best Israel ever had. It was their lack of devotion to God that caused their downfall.

A case can be made that Ahab did not completely reject Yahweh. He gave names to his children that confirmed his belief, and he did repent after the Naboth debacle. However, he allowed Jezebel to promote her own religion and import her gods. As for Jezebel, she was unsure of herself. She despised Elijah, but at the same time feared him as the only power opposing her and her god. She wanted him dead, and threatened him with death. This gave him the opportunity to escape. She wanted to prevent his influence, but did not want to give him martyr's status.

The challenge to the faith of Israel called for an Elijah. The survival of Yahwehism, despite the power of its opposition, testifies to God's reality and effectiveness. Three significant truths emerge from the story:

1. The emphasis on the exclusive worship of Yahweh as the only true God;
2. The enlargement of the dominion of Yahweh who directs all history and uses all people, even enemy nations, for His purpose;
3. The insistence on social justice as an absolute.

Without Moses, the Old Testament religion of Judaism would never have been born. Without Elijah, it would have died. Elijah has a prominent place in the three monotheistic religions of the world: Judaism, Christianity, and Islam.

In these chapters I am not trying to explain the Scriptures or extract a doctrine. Rather, I am endeavoring to take some narratives from the life of one biblical personality and see if they have certain applications for our time. God's Word was not only meant for those to whom it was first spoken/written, but also for us. Someone else might find other truths or applications than I have. That is the glory of the Scripture. A splendid example of the use of imaginative application is found in how G. Gerald Harrop uses the Naboth vineyard episode.

This study of the Elijah epoch began in 1980. Dr. William May and I were discussing the music ministry of the St. Charles Avenue Baptist Church in New Orleans. I suggested that we use Felix Mendelssohn's oratorio *Elijah* and a series of sermons to accompany the music. Together we selected themes and music. The series was presented in October 1980. The original five sermons are chapters 1, 2, 3, 5, and 10.

In 1983 the University Baptist Church of Hattiesburg, Mississippi, began planning for its twenty-fifth anniversary. I asked Dr. Thomas Porter if he and the choir would be interested in doing this. In addition to the five Sunday mornings, we added an evening concert to present the music as a whole.

Research in the New Orleans Baptist Theological Seminary library revealed that practically nothing had been done on Elijah, other than scholarly works in commentaries. There was virtually no homiletic material. What there was, was old; nothing contemporary. The most helpful was a book by Dr. B. Davie Napier, *Word of God, Word of Earth,* the Lyman Beecher Lectures on Preaching, given at Yale University in 1975. I have drawn heavily on Dr. Napier. Other sources have been noted where possible. Omissions of credit are unintentional. When one relies on memory, or fails to make proper notations, omissions do occur.

In these chapters I want the biblical narrative to be in the foreground. This does not mean that we shall always begin with the biblical narrative. Because the biblical material is limited, imagination must be used to enlarge and enlighten. Also, we need to see the scenes in some contemporary perspective. It is my desire that the reader shall have an experience that feels the impact of this man Elijah and have a sense of unity in the series of episodes.

I express appreciation to the staff of Broadman Press for their encouragement and helpful editorial assistance. I also express appreciation to Valerie Pierce for typing the manuscript—her fifth for me.

For any church that is interested, the sections of the Mendelssohn oratorio I have used are enclosed at the end of this book. The music was used in the morning service of worship, prior to the sermon.

For those interested in further reading, in addition to the biblical commentaries, I would suggest three books:

Davie Napier, *Word of God, Word of Earth* (Philadelphia: United Church Press, 1976); G. Gerald Harrop, *Elijah Speaks Today* (Nashville: Abingdon Press, 1975); and Aharon Wiener, *The Prophet Elijah in the Development of Judaism* (London: Routledge and Kegan, 1978).

G. AVERY LEE
New Orleans

1

A Personal Search for God

Let us use a mental time machine, transporting us back some twenty-eight centuries and finding ourselves in the ancient kingdom of Israel. A man named Ahab is the king. The Bible describes him as one who "did more to provoke the Lord, the God of Israel, to anger than all the kings of Israel who were before him" (1 Kings 16:33). Ahab's wife, Queen Jezebel, who was not an Israelite but a Sidonian, was so conspicuous for her evil-doing that her name has become a synonym for gross wickedness.

With Ahab's ascendency to the throne a new and alarming crisis invaded Israel's life. Hitherto the kings of Israel had promoted the inherited worship of Yahweh (Jehovah). Ahab made a new step. Following the precedent of Solomon, he allowed his foreign wives to build places of worship for their gods, and he "reared up an altar for Baal" (v. 32, KJV). If Jezebel had worshiped quietly, probably nothing would have happened. But Jezebel was different. No one could call her "irreligious"; she was most religious, but her religion was of the wrong kind.

Jezebel was a woman born to dominate. Burning

with evangelistic zeal and energetic, passionate, self-willed, and determined, she would stop at nothing to achieve her ends. Added to all this was a fanatical religious devotion. She believed her god must have at least an equal place with Israel's God.

Some will remember the name Claire Booth Luce. She was an outstanding playwright and the wife of Henry Luce, the founder of *Time* magazine. Mrs. Luce was converted to the Roman Catholic faith. President Franklin D. Roosevelt appointed her as ambassador to Italy. Mrs. Luce had an official appointment with the Pope. The story goes that after an hour, the Pope had a brief chance to speak and exclaimed: "But, Madame Ambassador, I *am* a Catholic!" Such zeal could describe Jezebel.

The people of Israel took no firm stand for or against God. In the crisis they were "limping between two sides" (1 Kings 18:21, ASV), not wanting to offend a soul, least of all Jezebel. And religious apathy and apostasy set in.

Into this situation a man named Elijah was called upon by God to act forcefully. As Shakespeare has Hamlet say:

> The time is out of joint; O cursed spite,
> That ever I was born to set it right.

Elijah was to set things right in Israel. But what were his credentials? We do not know. Virtually nothing is written about his background. He suddenly appeared before King Ahab and announced that a severe drought was on the way. Then, as quickly, he disappeared.

To face Ahab and Jezebel, Elijah needed to hear more than "Elijah! get thee hence." Elijah believed in God, no doubt about that. He had faith, but he needed fact—the reality of God—before tackling a tough task. He needed the confidence of:

> He shall give his angels charge over thee;
> They shall . . . guide . . . protect thee."

Elijah's forecast of "no rain" stretched into three years, and the drought was ruining the nation's economy. A man named Obadiah is introduced into the narrative. In the oratorio *Elijah,* Mendelssohn has Obadiah sing some words of the prophet Joel:

> Ye people, rend your hearts, and not your garments, for your transgressions the prophet Elijah hath sealed the heavens through the word of God. I therefore say to ye, Forsake your idols, return to God.

But how were they to find God and return to Him? The cry,

> Oh! that I knew where I might find Him, . . .

was answered with:

> If with all your hearts ye truly seek Me, ye shall ever surely find Me." Thus saith our God.

Where to find and verify God is a necessity as serious for us as it was for the people of Israel in Elijah's generation.

If nothing else can characterize my fifty years' ministry, this chapter declares what I have tried to do and encourage others to do—*engage in a personal search for God.*

I have never doubted the fact of God. At times I have sensed the "presence" of God. I believe I was called by God to preach the gospel. I have felt I was doing God's will in the right place; imperfectly, and not always at my best, but trying. There have been times when I have fretted and fumed inwardly, and occasionally I have felt frustrated. I have never spoken the words, "Oh! that I knew where I might find Him," in a mood of depression, but I have often spoken those words in a mood of haunting desire. There was no feeling that God was lost from me, but perhaps I had distanced myself from Him and needed some reassurance or reaffirmation that I was at least headed in the right direction.

This personal hunger for God has been for me to know more and to understand God better, so I could share and thus better enable others to quest for themselves. I have shared the uncertainties as well as the certainties in an open and honest effort. No one knows everything about God, and no one has a monopoly on God. There is always more about God than any one of us or any group grasps.

I have never insisted that anyone believe exactly as I do about God, the Lord Jesus Christ, the Christian faith, or my Baptist heritage. I have asked people to commit themselves to God through faith in Jesus Christ that begins the Christian journey, and then to learn and mature as they go along.

In one sense God is not a matter of *faith,* but a matter of *fact.* The trouble with many is not that they think God is *untrue,* but they feel Him *unreal.* It is one matter to believe in God, as almost everyone does; it is another matter to confront God as inescapable reality. Indeed, in any realm it is one kind of experience to believe in anything, and it is altogether another kind of experience to discover it real.

For example, we all believed in love before we ourselves fell in love. We read about love, saw it depicted in movies and TV, and watched our parents or some of our peers demonstrating love. We believed in love. Then one day we ourselves fell in love, profoundly and abidingly in love, and this abstract in which we had believed became real to us. What was faith became fact.

So far as belief in God's existence is concerned, practically everyone is a "believer." We could as easily think that the musical notes fell fortuitously together in Mendelssohn's oratorio as to believe that this vast, amazing universe created and arranged itself. No, most of us are not atheists, but that is about as far as many go. God is not real to them. Once in awhile, when some mighty experience shakes us to the depths, God may seem real. But, for the most part, to multitudes of people God is only a matter of opinion and belief, not experience.

Whatever is real to us, emotionally vivid, and confidently assured, becomes morally controlling. Wherever anything happens on this earth for the good of people, something has become real to somebody. You see, it is not the things we theoretically believe that make the difference so much as it is the things that are real to us. In our present situation we do not need more people with more beliefs and opinions about social justice, human rights, and international peace. There are many of us who believe in all of those causes. We must

have people to whom such issues are so real they can
do no other than to live, and perhaps die, for them. And
we have a few who are like that.

But here, alas, is also a source of hypocrisy: to
claim we believe in one thing when another thing is real
to us.

Here is a man playing the success-money-rise-to-
the-top game with whatever manipulation or ruthless-
ness he thinks he can get away with. Let him aver as
often as he wants, "I believe in God and Jesus Christ,"
but something else is real to him.

"I believe in God and Christianity," testifies one
woman. Yet look at her! A detached bystander can see
that not Christian living but social ambition is her
dominant motive. She is a social climber. Above all else
on earth she wants to walk in what she regards as the
"preferred circles" in the community. She is trying to
crash the gate. Let her repeat all the creeds of Christen-
dom—what is real to her is something else.

Or a preacher, not honestly interested in speaking
and sharing the gospel truth as he sees and understands
it, but anxious to curry popular favor and be the "pet
lamb" of the congregation, or to play safe ecclesiastical
politics so he can rise to leadership and power. Let him
repeat all the shibboleths of orthodoxy; something else
is real to him.

The reality of the gospel is often strangled and
muted by such men, women, and preachers. This is not
to indicate that a successful businessman cannot be a
Christian or a socially active woman or a religious lead-
er cannot be truly Christian. They can, and they are!

But I emphasize that what is real to them dominates them—and us.

When Jesus said: "Blessed are the pure in heart, for they shall see God" (Matt. 5:8), that was a strange condition to lay down as a prerequisite to seeing God. No one of us would ever have dreamed of making a statement like that. More likely we would say, "If one is to know God, one must have the grasp of a philosophic mind," but they would not talk about a pure heart. Indeed, if we are looking for God off somewhere in the stars, or seek to find Him at the end of a metaphysical argument, then what does being pure in heart have to do with that? But not only Jesus, the psalmist and the prophets stressed the same truth.

Jesus put a child before His disciples and noted, "Of such is the kingdom of God" (Mark 10:14, KJV). To find the Divine in a child requires a clean heart—clean from sophistication, cynicism, and unkindness.

> Jesus went out into nature and said, "Consider the lilies ... Solomon in all his glory was not arrayed like one of these... God so clothes the grass" (Matt. 6:28-30). To find God in lilies and grass takes a clean heart.

> Jesus came upon Peter, James, and John—ordinary men in whom commonplace eyes would never have seen anything but commonplace things, but Jesus discovered in them divine possibilities and brought them out. To find divine things in common people takes a clean heart—clean from contemptuousness, scorn, and derision.

> Jesus went out into a social situation full of injustice and into an ecclesiastical situation full of conventionality and corruption, where acquiescence

on His part would have been safe and easy. To hear
God calling us out of evil situations takes a clean
heart.

You see, Jesus was not doing what we do—looking
for God somewhere off among the stars or trying to find
Him at the end of some philosophical dialogue. He was
seeing God. Do we get that? *Seeing* God in children and
nature and plain people, in ordinary situations and opportunities for service. My soul! Let's stop arguing
about God for a moment, and sit down before the towering fact that the real God takes eyes to see.

Of course, the real *anything* takes eyes to see.
"Blessed are the pure in heart, for they shall see" (Matt.
5:8). We could stop the Beatitude right there. They shall
see friendship, beauty, goodness, love—*God!* All such
truths take eyes to see. Michaelangelo's real *Moses* or
David or *Pieta* or the Sistine Chapel do not lie at the end
of an argument; they take eyes to see. A lasting friendship does not lie at the end of a long search; it takes eyes
to see, to experience, to peer deeply into what is real in
another person. A tourist observed:

> I stood once on a noble slope of the Alps on one of those
> priceless days when the autumnal coloring was just begin-
> ning to appear and, wrapped in silence amid the majesty
> of the mountains, I saw two of my countrymen steaming
> up beside me. One called out, "We have heard there is a
> great view somewhere up here. Where is it?" What was the
> use of explaining? There it was but it took eyes to see.

People everywhere search for God, discussing and
philosophizing about God. I do not ask that we cease
that; rather I urge us to go beyond that. Suppose we did
discover the God for whom we are searching at the end

of our discussions, what good would that do? Many people have argued themselves into believing in God and then discovered that it made little difference in their lives, for they did not see this deeper matter:

> . . . Earth's crammed with heaven.
> And every common bush afire with God;
> But only he who sees takes off his shoes.

Some of you may think that this chapter is missing the mark of the subject, or is a long way off from the hectic hurly-burly of our distracted time. If anyone thinks that, that someone needs this truth, for he/she is all turned around. It is easy enough to be like that in ordinary times. It is easier in these troubled days. We believe in God. Yes! But we are still turned around. The spiritual values which give us our direction, so we know which way we ought to go in our confused time, are not real to us—we have trouble seeing.

The essence of the matter is this: There is no religion which amounts to much except that which is to be found in people to whom God is real. The older I grow the more interest I have in that. Of course, I believe that Christianity offers us the best and the most there is to know about God. Jesus Christ is the way and the truth and the life (see John 14:6).

There are times in our lives and periods in history when the irreligious people seem to have all of the powerful arguments. The most convincing facts seem to be on their side. The reasons for not believing seem distressingly more evident than do the assurances of faith. There are times like that, despite the reassuring hymns we sing in church. To all outward appearances God

seems to be nowhere near, or, at best, too remote and
far away to make any difference. Someone once said
that if the skeptics were wise they would look to the
Bible for their arguments. How often in its pages we
hear voices speaking in bewilderment, half in anger, half
in anguish: "Where are you, God? Why do you hide
your face? Why are you silent when the impious swal-
low up the good? O, that I knew where I might find
him!"

We are living in a day when such taunts haunt us.
Even in ordinary times it is not easy to maintain a
constant awareness of God in our lives. We have
enough personal disappointments to raise such questions. But when these personal frustrations become general and are set in a generation like ours, where one
towering frustration after another seems to overshadow
the whole world, a mood is created which none of us can
escape. Today there is an atmosphere of gloom that
engulfs us like a fog,

> Blacker than a hundred midnights
> Down in a cypress swamp.[1]

Where can we look to find our bearings, discover
some word of encouragement, and hear if God is speaking? When we cry: "Oh, that I knew where I might find
him," verification of the reality of God comes when we
believe: "If with all your hearts ye truly seek me, Ye
shall ever surely find me. Thus saith our God."

Heavenly Father, we know You can be found, for You have sought us ever since Eden. You are not far off; we are. You are not reluctant to be found; we are slow to seek. But there are times when Your exact location is uncertain, when Your directions seem mumbled, and we can't understand. But we are aware that You have made Yourself known in Jesus Christ, and we can respond to and follow Him. And this we would do. Amen.

2

In Finding and Following God, What Do We Get?

1 Kings 17:8-24

In numerous ways, this is a ghastly time to be alive. In many more ways, this is a great time to be alive.

The future is coming, but only we can decide where it is going. And this isn't 100 percent true. There are some marvelous and exciting prospects ahead. But along with every benefit will come a whole set of new problems. And while we do not have full control over where the future will go, we do have plenty to say about our part in it and our attitude toward it. Collectively, we all have some responsibility for the future. It doesn't simply *happen* to us; someone is responsible for it. We must learn all we can from the past and use it to help us tomorrow.

The human race is now making choices that will determine our long-term future. No one knows the precise nature of those choices, but futurists agree that today's actions will reverberate throughout the years ahead. There's not much originality in that. So, I repeat: in many ways, this is a ghastly time to be alive. In many more ways it is a great time to be alive. And I choose to emphasize the latter.

When I hear someone say, "Find God's will for your life, then do it, and all will be well," I believe that, although it is not as easy and simple as it sounds, nor does it mean that everything is going to be all right. When I see those motto stickers, "Christ Is the Answer," I believe that, although all questions are not answered nor are all problems solved. Sometimes when we ask questions and receive answers, we need to question the answers. When I read Dante's lines, "In His will is our peace," I believe that, although life is not always peaceable. In all three of these beliefs I live in an uneasy questioning. Too much of the time such "preachments" are pronounced as if doing the will of God and taking Christ as the answer makes everything all right, gives all the answers, and ushers in tranquillity. And that doesn't always happen. Life is not always tranquil, some answers never come, and trying to do God's will doesn't always make all things right.

One day Peter said to Jesus, "We have left everything and followed you" (Mark 10:28). The implication is: *"Now what shall we get? What's in it for us?"* Jesus answered:

> Truly, I say to you, there is no one who has left house or brother or sisters or mother or father or children or lands, for my sake and for the gospel, who will not receive a hundredfold now in this time, houses and brothers and sisters and mothers and children and lands, with persecutions, and in the age to come eternal life (vv. 29-30).

It is simple for us to overlook two words—"with persecutions": trouble, not tranquillity.

If ever a man followed the will of God it was Paul. Listen to his autobiography:

> Five times I have received . . . forty lashes less one. Three times I have been beaten with rods, once I was stoned. Three times I have been shipwrecked; a day and a night I have been adrift at sea; on frequent journeys, in danger from rivers, danger from robbers, danger from my own people, danger from Gentiles, danger in the city, danger in the wilderness, danger at sea, danger from false brethren; in toil and hardship, through many a sleepless night, in hunger and thirst, often without food, in cold and exposure (2 Cor. 11:24-27).

Then this same Paul wrote:

> We rejoice in our sufferings, knowing that suffering produces endurance, and endurance produces character, and character produces hope, and hope does not disappoint us, because God's love has been poured into our hearts through the Holy Spirit which has been given to us (Rom. 5:3-5).

While at times I've skirted the edges of this seeming contradiction, I do not feel I've adequately dealt with it. I've long needed to preach such a sermon to myself about trusting God. Maybe it's not too late, even after fifty years of preaching. While I do trust God, and have since childhood, there is an uncomfortable feeling that I neither fully understand nor practice such trust. Perhaps you share my suspicions that often, when we state that we trust God, we actually mean we trust ourselves, or others, or else, driven by circumstances to desperation, we "leave it in God's hands," with a feeling of *un*expectancy that He is likely to come to our aid in a convincing manner.

Elijah, was one of the key figures in Israel's long history—a man perhaps second only to Moses in Old Testament Judaistic importance, one whose career had many parallels to Moses. Almost thirty centuries later, Elijah still has a prominent place in Judaism, for every time the Passover is observed a place is reserved for Elijah, who is expected to be present.

In the episode we consider here, God told Elijah to go to the brook Cherith. So Elijah left wherever he had been. We don't know where he came from, or even where he was when he turned toward Cherith to be sustained by ravens and a drying-up creek. But he responded to the call of God and went. And that took *trust*—where survival, to eat or not to eat, depended upon capricious ravens. We need to recover that lost virtue of trust.

Sometimes, not often but sometimes, a pastor "takes a cut" in pay when he changes churches. And pastors in my denomination are dependent upon "ravens" who can cut off their supply at any time. In fact, an estimated 2,500 ministers of my denomination face forced terminations every year. Their "brook of Cherith" dries up, and the ravens cut off their supply. You see, not every call of God to service is *up*—in either pay, prestige, or permanence.

In Elijah's case the ravens stopped feeding him, and the creek dried up, even though he was doing God's will.

There was little improvement in God's next call for him to go to Zarapeth. The resources of the ravens and the creek were replaced by the dubious, tenuous hospitality of a poverty-stricken unnamed widow. But Elijah did as he was instructed. There is always some absurdity in every act of faith; to live in the assumption that, if there is no food, the ravens will bring it, or a poor widow, who can barely meet her own needs and those of her son, will share what little she has.

Then the woman's son became sick and died. So, although Elijah was doing God's will, matters were not turning out right. There were more questions than answers, more disturbance than tranquillity.

There is a lesson to be learned here, and it is: If there is work to do, we must do it, and not leave everything to God. We have grown accustomed to and comfortable with "God works in all things—even in history." The real worker in this episode was Elijah himself. However, human work does not exclude Divine work. Human action is often made effective by "something beyond" the human's working in cooperation. Too many of us try to excuse ourselves with a piety which does not even say, "Let George do it," but says, "Let God do it."

Elijah, taking matters into his own hands upon the death of the lad, was neither the first nor the last to have a controversy with God. Listen to some of them:

> *Moses:* Why did you treat your servant so badly? (Num. 11:11-14).

> *Job:* Why do you rear man at all, or pay any mind to him? Inspect him every morning, test him every moment? Will you never look away from me? Leave me till I swallow my spittle (Job 7:17-19).

> *Jeremiah:* Yahweh, you have deceived me (Jer. 20:7-9).

Habakkuk: How long, Yahweh, am I to cry for help
while you will not listen (Hab. 1:2).

So Elijah cried in a brief, incredulous prayer, charged with resentment and outrage, as he feared the child was dead. An ancient and authentic wording of the prayer is that of exasperation and anguish of spirit. Dr. Napier translates 1 Kings 17:20:

My God, can it be your intention, in addition (to the drought and attendant disaster) to inflict catastrophe on the very widow, who has opened her home to me, by killing her son?[1]

In other words:

Are you really going to go through with this? As if privation is not enough, can you bring totally undeserved judgment on this child and his mother by taking his life, leaving her in grief, and me in contempt and rejection? My God, Yahweh!

The child lived. Renewed life had occurred. First Kings 17:21 indicates that Elijah used a form of coronary pulmonary resuscitation: "Then he stretched himself upon the child three times, and cried to the Lord, 'O Lord my God, let this child's soul come into him again.'"

The child revived. Elijah gave the child back to his mother and exclaimed: "See, your son lives." And she responded: "Now I know that you are a man of God, and that the word of Yahweh [that you speak] is truth" (vv. 23-24).

Remember that earlier lesson I mentioned: if there is work to do we must do it? Well, there is another part of that lesson—in doing something we run the risk of failure, as well as the risk of succeeding.

These episodes are a study in the relationship between produce and providence. Elijah heard the divine call to hide himself by the brook Cherith. The brook dried up. But its drying led him to new opportunities and resources. Following God's leadership, Elijah was guided from the problem of saving his own life to the privilege of saving a widow's faith and her son's life. The widow thought that this man had brought to light some hidden sin, of which she was unaware, and that the untimely death of her son was the punishment. Such a primitive idea of God as one who seeks out unwitting or long-forgotten sins, and is fervent in dealing out strict penalties, is far from dead. And some preachers play on it to increase guilt and bring a conversion. How often we hear: "What have I done to deserve this?" A poignant scene in *Fiddler on the Roof* illustrates. Tevyeh's horse has gone lame and he speaks to God: "Why my horse? Me, I could understand, but why my horse? She's done nothing to deserve this."

In contrast, Elijah regarded the boy's death as an act of arbitrary injustice on the part of God. This had happened to the very widow whom God Himself had chosen. As if she didn't have enough anxiety and privation in the general disaster of her own poverty, God added this extra burden of grief. And Elijah wouldn't take that! The idea that thinks in terms of God's arbitrariness rather than justice (or mercy/love) was sometimes prevalent in the ninth century BC, and it is not totally dead in the twentieth century AD. It is remarkable that Elijah questioned at all. In addition to emphasizing the miracle aspect of the story, it is important that we see Elijah on the scene with some understanding, ability, and willingness to do something.

One of the knotty problems we face is in seeing people, not en masse, but as individuals. For example, we may intellectualize about the problem of "battered children" and quote the statistics, shaking our heads in dismay. But when we see *just one battered child* we are apt to be triggered into some action.

During the Civil War, Senator Charles Sumner, absorbed in his grand plans for the abolition of slavery, was asked by Julia Ward Howe (who wrote "The Battle Hymn of the Republic") to meet some friends who had suffered because of slavery. He declined, pontificating in a lofty manner: "Really, Julia, I have lost all interest in individuals." She answered: "Why, Charles, God hasn't got as far as that yet."

When we protest that we can't do anything about the vast problems of the world, we are right. But we can do something for one person. My person may not be your person, nor yours mine. Most of us spend our lives among ordinary people in common, everyday tasks. In such ordinary circumstances we can offer that cup of water in Jesus' name.

It would have been easy for Elijah, facing a nation-wide drought and living under the oppressive rule of Ahab and Jezebel, to have been a Charles Sumner so absorbed in his own plans to topple Ahab that he had no time for a widow, alibiing: "It's too bad about the boy." Instead, Elijah approached God Himself in trying to do something.

Many people, looking on this bloody shambles of

a world, find it hard to believe in God. If this world were
not in a mess, I would find it hard *to* believe in God. So!
If this is God's world, it is morally law-abiding. In such
a world if we, the nations and people of the world, break
all the conditions that make peace and brotherhood
possible, and fulfill the conditions that make disturbance and war inevitable, then the agony we suffer is not
a denial of God, but an affirmation of the existence of
a God of moral law in whose world what we sow is what
we reap. Ahab and Jezebel had sown, and God was at
work to bring them their harvest.

Time was when one of us could be sent on a mission by our government and go in confidence. Once an
English colonel was sent on a hazardous assignment to
Tibet. The mission was full of dangers, yet he moved
among them with serenity. When asked how he could
be so calm, he replied:

> It is twofold: First, I have been sent by unimpeachable
> authority for a purpose which is sound; second, if I get in
> a tight place, I have the government behind me, which
> would use all its resources to see me through.

Time was when one could make that statement,
but can we make it these days? More likely we would
hear before we were sent: "The agency will disavow any
knowledge of you."

There is an obscure verse in Exodus 20:21, "And
Moses drew near unto the thick darkness where God
was" (KJV).

What a place to find God! Most of us would more
naturally expect to find God in life's lovely experiences.
"Praise God, from whom all blessings flow" is where we

expect to find God—in our blessings. But when disaster and darkness come we commonly implore: "Where is God? Oh! that I knew where I might find him."

We are on a time machine shuttling back and forth over a thirty-century period between someplace in the United States and an obscure village called Zarapeth and a brook named Cherith, where a man named Elijah, following the leadership of God, found himself in darkness, wondering where God was. In the shuttling we learn that that scene is here with us today. We find God in life's loveliness, to be sure. But sooner or later each of us comes to the place where, if we are to find God at all, we must find Him in some wilderness. Not only does life land us in some unpromising situations, but our whole earth is desperately tragic.

As a matter of fact, many of the most memorable encounters with God have been found in this "thick darkness." Moses in the desert, Isaiah in Babylon with his exiled people, Job, out of his calamity, saying: "I have heard of thee by the hearing of the ear: but now mine eye seeth thee" (Job 42:5, KJV). And Calvary. My soul, crucifixion isn't lovely! Who, casually looking on that day, would have thought God was there? Even Jesus felt God's absence. But countless millions since have found God there. "At Calvary!"

There are many personal thick darknesses here, dried up creeks of Cherith: An alcoholic or drug hell, the death of a child or a loved one, the breakup of a home/family, or another personal breakdown. I don't know a real darkness experience, but I've been through some awfully shadowy ones, and I do know that some of life's most revealing insights do come from such difficulty.

What went on inside Elijah that made possible his discovery of God?

For one, in finding God he found something about which to be angry: the situation in Israel caused by Ahab and Jezebel and the death of a boy. He was angry at something unbearably wrong. That was the beginning. His anger needed harnessing, but it was basic to all that followed. His indignation against evil got him somewhere. *But where?*

In the movie, *Network,* there is a dramatic scene where the executive throws open his window and shouts, "I'm mad! And I'm not going to take it anymore."

Look at our world! "It is hard to find God here," you say. Well, we can start looking, can't we? We can see evil that ought to arouse our indignation. We can at least quit our moral apathy and wake up to some issues of right and wrong.

This start led Elijah to a second stage. In finding God, Elijah was confronted with *Elijah.* He had never before taken a searching look at himself. Outward wrongs were there demanding that someone set them right. But if Elijah were to be the one, he had to tackle Elijah first. To confront oneself in the "thick darkness," to be told there is Divine opportunity, is a soul-searching experience.

Of course, Elijah backed off from that. Who was he, an obscure prophet, to do anything about the situation the king had caused? Of course, he shrank from such a formidable cause, at first—but not finally. He confronted himself until he dedicated himself and found his vocation. By God's help, he would be Elijah.

We come to grips with the central theme, however, when we follow Elijah's experiences to a deeper level. In this encounter of right against wrong, in this self-dedication for his people's sake, he came face to face with God in an unlikely place. Whatever may have been his idea of God, he at least expected to meet up with God at Cherith or Zarapeth. Wasn't that where God had told him to go? But what kind of situations were poverty and death in which to meet God?

Many of us are in precisely that state of mind. We habitually talk of God in terms of love, goodness, and mercy, so that when we face a situation in our personal experience where these virtues are singularly absent, we lose all sense of God. "Where is He?" we ask.

Looking at the present dark world, let's shuttle back only two centuries. Think of the calamitous era of the American Revolution, so terrific that many then could perceive of nothing but chaos and calamity. Yet, beneath the surface, see what was going on. The thirteen colonies had been for years at odds, sometimes at swords' points with one another. Then in 1774, at the First Continental Congress, Patrick Henry of Virginia made a speech in which he said:

> Throughout the continent government is dissolved. Landmarks are dissolved. Where are now your boundaries? The distinction between Virginians, Pennsylvanians, New Yorkers, New Englanders are no more. I am not a Virginian, I am an American.

See what was going on there for those with eyes to

perceive. A nation was being born. An historian describing that scene exclaimed: "Forty three delegates
sat spellbound, hypnotized altogether. It was crazy
what they had just heard; they knew it; *an American,*
in God's name what was that?"

But Patrick Henry was right. He would be right
again if he could be here with us and, beneath all of our
seething turmoil, could see the emergence of new germinative ideas of world unity, world citizenship, world
brotherhood. This era of ours, though dark wilderness,
is also *holy ground.* Let's play our part in it, large or
small, against the little-mindedness, the prejudices, the
hatreds that individuals, neighbors, races, and nations
have. When Rip Van Winkle went to sleep the sign on
his favorite inn was George III; when he woke up the
sign read "George Washington Slept Here." Rip had
slept through a revolution. We must not do that now.
Rather, let us remember that line from "America the
Beautiful":

> O beautiful for heroes proved
> In liberating strife.

God is here. Liberation can also be here, if we work
together with God.

When anyone finds God in an unlikely place we
may be fairly sure that God was earlier found in some
likely place. Some beauty touched our life, some love
blessed us, some friend trusted us, some goodness made
us aware of God. Don't miss that, for it's not easy to
find God in the hard places. Start trying to find Him in
the likely places. Beauty, goodness, and loveliness are
here; nobility of character, unselfish service, moral

courage, and lives through which Divine light shines are here; and Jesus Christ is here, too, full of grace and truth, in whom we see the light of the knowledge of the glory of God.

Find God in these bright places, that you may also find Him in the "thick darkness."

In finding and following God what comes to us?—not always serenity but always the assurance that God is with us. We hear the call of God to go someplace and do something. We respond, taking the risk of failure, as well as the risk of success, and we are not always successful. But the risk and the adventure are worth taking.

In many ways, this is a ghastly time to be alive. In many more ways, this is a great time to be alive. And I choose to emphasize the latter. "Now Cherith's brook is dried up, Elijah, arise and depart, and get thee to Zarapeth; . . . Blessed are the men who fear Him; They ever walk in the ways of peace."

Heavenly Father, we do want to follow You, but where we want to go often conflicts with what we think You want, so we hesitate and sometimes strike out in the opposite direction. Maybe we feel that following You is no flower-strewn path because we see what happened to Elijah, and we just don't want to take the risk. We need a clearer vision and a keener sense of what it is to really trust You. Surely, it is Your will that we follow Jesus Christ, else You wouldn't have sent Him. So we pray for the grit of determination to place our hands in those nail-scarred hands and exclaim, "Lead on! We follow."

3

Affirming Who Is to Be God—I
1 Kings 18

A man named Hans Denk lived a long time ago. He wrote:

> O my God, how does it happen in this poor old world that Thou art so great and yet nobody finds Thee; that Thou callest so loudly and nobody hears Thee; that Thou art so near and nobody feels Thee; and Thou givest Thyself to everybody and nobody knows Thy name? Men flee from Thee and say they cannot see Thee; they stop their ears and say they cannot hear Thee.

That describes King Ahab of whom the Bible says "did more to provoke the Lord God of Israel, . . . than all the kings of Israel who were before him" (1 Kings 16:33).

That is Queen Jezebel who brought in her false religion, set up her sycophant priests of Baal, and was so conspicuous in her evildoing that her name has become a synonym for perfidious wickedness.

That is the people of Israel wanting it both ways, afraid of God and terrified by Jezebel, limping from one altar of worship to the other with no real belief in or conviction about either, but not wanting to antagonize either.

That, too, is Elijah, searching for God, disturbing the uneasy status quo peace by pronouncing an extended drought, and challenging king, queen, priests, and people.

As the late Walt Kelly's Pogo once opined: "We have seen the enemy, and he is *us.*" We look for God with our backs toward Him and protest we can't see Him. We stop our ears and claim we can't hear Him. In our confusion we don't know His name; so we give our allegiance to a variety of Baals.

One of the most dramatic, compelling scenes in the Bible is Elijah's confrontation with the priests of Baal on Mount Carmel. The sheer, raw courage of one prophet of God pitting himself against 450 priests of Baal, backed up by the power of royalty, makes for all the intensity of a shoot-out at the old corral of No Name City.

Mount Carmel rises out of the sea at the western end of the Valley of Esdraelon. It is not high, as mountains go, only 1,810 feet. But rising as it does from the plains it is awesome. Today at the foot of Mount Carmel lies the chief port of modern Israel, the city of Haifa. About halfway up is the golden-domed temple of the international headquarters of the Bahai faith. So modern Carmel also has its religious conflict because the Bahais are suffering persecution in Iran.

Let's use our time capsule again and go back to the Mount Carmel of some thirty centuries ago. Ahab was the king of Israel. His queen was Jezebel. To understate the case, neither of them was greatly admired by the biblical writers. Suddenly, from out of nowhere, and with no explanation as to how an obscure man could come before a king, Elijah roared:

> As the Lord God of Israel lives, before whom I stand, there shall be neither dew nor rain these years, except by my word (1 Kings 17:1).

Can you imagine a man praying for it not to rain in a land where water is a precious commodity? Can you imagine a modern sycophant speaking like that to the president of the United States or to the premier of the Soviet Union? Would that someone would! And it did not rain for three and one-half years. The story is ingrained in Israel's history. Micah spoke of it. Jesus referred to it, and so did the writer of the Epistle of James.

As the Carmel episode begins, Ahab had an "APB" out on Elijah. Subpoenas were in hand to bring him in. But Elijah evaded apprehension, appeared on his own, and told Ahab to gather the people on the slopes of Mount Carmel. Why didn't Ahab seize him and execute him right then and there? Instead, Ahab called together 450 priests of Baal. When the people were assembled, Elijah made his memorable demand for the people to determine who was to be God:

> How long will you go limping with two different opinions? If the Lord is God, follow him; but if Baal, then follow him. And the people did not answer him a word (1 Kings 18:21).

Their silence was partly shame and partly indecision, mixed with loads of fear. It's not easy to be an open Christian in today's Russia or China, for example. I have a Korean preacher friend, Jin Hwa Hong, who was pastor of the Korean Baptist Church in New Orleans. He told me that he often preached in Seoul with government spies sitting in the congregation with their tape recorders. And there are Christian preachers in South Korean jails right now.

The King James version uses the word "halt," which means indecision.

The Revised Standard Version uses "limping," indicating insecurity because of an injury.

The New English Bible uses "sit on the fence," which is a playing of both sides so as not to antagonize anyone, least of all Jezebel.

Our English slang has a word, *mugwump,* which means "a bolter from the Republican party . . . an independent." A later wag described a mugwump as "one who sits on a fence with his mug on one side and his wump on the other." But he who sits on a fence gets his tail in a crack and is pinched from both sides!

Elijah then challenged the priests of Baal to a trial by fire. Two altars were to be built and two offerings laid upon them. The priests were to pray to Baal and Elijah to Yahweh. If the prayers of the 450 priests were answered by the coming down of fire to consume the altar and the offering, that would show Baal was God. But if Elijah's prayer brought down the fire, that would prove Yahweh was God.

From sunrise till noon Mount Carmel echoed their cries: "Baal, hear us" (v. 26, KJV). There was no answer. Nothing happened. No fire. During a moment of quiet, Elijah, standing on the other side, mocked them with some of the most exquisite satire found in all literature: "Cry aloud, for he is a god; either he is musing, or perhaps he has gone aside (v. 27).

The language of the Hebrew is plain, indicating that "gone aside" could mean "answered the call of nature."

The Baalites were stirred to renewed efforts and fervor, and once again Carmel rang with their frenzied shouts. The guttural sounds of the Middle Eastern languages make for a high decibel level. Late in the afternoon they gave up.

Now it was Elijah's turn. In quiet contrast he repaired the long-neglected altar of God. Around the altar he dug a trench and drenched the altar with water, four barrels of precious water. Why, the man must have been out of his mind! Seeing water wasted must have caused anguished wails. Then, in one of those sudden hushes that often descend upon a crowd, Elijah prayed:

> O Lord, God of Abraham, and Isaac, and Israel, let it be known that this day thou art God in Israel, and that I am thy servant, and that I have done these things at thy word. Answer me, O Lord, answer me, that this people may know that thou, O Lord, art God, and that thou hast turned their hearts back (vv. 36-37).

Elijah's prayer was finished. Fire came from heaven, consumed the sacrifice and the altar, and licked up the water in the trenches.

Some have tried to give a natural explanation of God answering by fire. However, even trying to give a natural explanation does not lessen the effect. The point of the story is that the lightning, if it were lightning, came at that particular time. Let's not become bogged down about natural causes versus supernatural miracle. The significant fact is that *something happened* to show that God was superior to Baal. Micah, Jesus, and James remembered it hundreds of years later, and we are talking about it today. When the people saw what happened, they fell on their knees and cried: "The Lord, he is God" (v. 39).

Choice is a constant, never-settled matter. Today is a time of decision for both nations and individuals, just as it has always been. The choice made by those before us is not binding on us, although we are having to suffer the consequences and are trying to undo certain wrong choices of the past. The past has always led to the present. We hear many sermons about the sins of the fathers being visited on the children. Why can't we say as much for the virtues of the fathers? We do have many virtues in our heritage. Why can't we emphasize those virtues in the future directions we choose to go?

That a choice is urgent need not be labored. We are painfully aware that something is wrong with our world and the people in it. Most of us do not desire to continue going in the direction we are headed because we fear the ultimate destination.

It has been felt for years that the church is not adequately affecting society, and there is a general apathy in nations once considered to be Christian. It is disturbing to see the rapid rise of militant antiChristian movements. We are faced with a situation similar to that of Elijah at Mount Carmel. People not formally denying God but practically worshiping Baal.

In the beginning, in Eden, everything revolved around Adam and Eve choosing for themselves and assuming the responsibility for their choice. Choice always implies the possibility of rejection. If a choice can be accepted it can also be declined. To meet Jesus Christ is to stand at the forks of a road, to desire all that He offers, and be done with all that offends Him. The two aspects of the act of positive response to Jesus are called repentance and faith: repentance, turning from the road that leads away from Him; faith, the commitment to the road that leads toward Him.

The climax of Elijah's conflict was yet to come. Even after the victory, the three and one-half year drought in the nation did not immediately end. Elijah and a young man climbed to the top of Mount Carmel to see if the rain was on its way. "Go up now, look toward the sea," Elijah said to the young man. But nowhere could he see what Elijah wanted. "There is nothing," he reported. "Go again seven times" (vv. 43-44). Elijah kept praying while the youth kept looking. Finally, on the seventh look, he came rushing back, excitedly: "Behold, a little cloud like a man's hand!"

In a little while that cloud expanded until it covered the heavens. The wind came sweeping in from the sea, and there was "a sound of abundance of rain" (v. 41).

> Thanks be to God, He laveth the thirsty land. The waters gather, they rush along.

You see, even when we do decide about God, all of our problems are not immediately solved. Some of them never are in this life. I saw a cartoon of a confused man saying: "Just when I learn the answers, they change the questions."

It took a while for the rain to come. The problem of the drought was solved, but another issue reared its head. Evil never takes defeat lying down but always plots a new course of action. This requires eternal vigilance on our part.

Jezebel, in a rage, tore out after Elijah. She would have his hide! And in the meantime, there was that sordid episode of Ahab coveting a piece of property owned by Naboth and Jezebel's conniving deceit to help Ahab steal it. Evil is never satisfied with what it has; it always wants more—*all*!

But there is always the "cloud" that is the promise. On the horizon of our dismal moral drought there are some such clouds. A pessimist might muse that these clouds are a portent of trouble. I prefer the optimistic view.

There is still a ray of hope that the U.S.-Russian Summits might work, despite the turmoil around the world.

We have tackled such problems as human and civil rights, poverty, and ecology in a head-on manner. In all these areas there is much to be done, but there has been a start.

Religiously, there is no massive return to the church, no dramatic religious awakening. And it causes me concern that in our own churches there are members who limp, absent themselves from church, and give it no support. But the attendance, participation, and support of those who do share is encouraging.

On the world scene—in Indonesia, South Korea, Brazil, Africa, and elsewhere—the response to the Christian message is hearty.

Clouds no bigger than a man's hand? Yes, *but clouds!* and clouds speak the promise of abundant rain.

So, there is Mount Carmel, a constant reminder that we must affirm who is to be our God. I must make that decision, so must you. And we can't do that with our backs turned toward Him, with our eyes and ears stopped up. I plead with you to say: "The Lord, He is God, I will serve Him."

Heavenly Father, that we must have a god to whom we give allegiance is inescapable. But what god? Too many among us have chased after strange and false Baals, even though we know You are the only God. We believe that, but our actions belie our beliefs. We are not having a contest, nor are we asking for a supernatural demonstration; we've had enough of that. After all, You have shown Yourself in Jesus Christ; what more do we need? In this quiet moment, we would decide that You are to be our God through our faith in Jesus Christ.

4

Affirming Who Is to Be God—II

1 Kings 18; Acts 17:22-34

In Chaim Potok's novel, *The Book of Lights,* there
is a scene where a Jewish chaplain and his Catholic
assistant observe a Japanese praying in a temple in
Kyoto:

> "Do you think God is listening to him, John?"
> "I don't know, chappie, I never thought of it."
> "Neither did I until now. If He's not listening, why
> not? If He is, then—well, what are we all about,
> John?"[1]

On several occasions in the city of Athens, I have
stood on the small knoll known as Mars Hill and have
looked up toward the Acropolis on which stands the
Parthenon. My awe is only slightly less than that of
Paul. When Paul first saw the Parthenon it was then
nearly five hundred years old. On today's Mars Hill is
a bronze plaque on which is engraved in Greek Paul's
speech which begins: "Men of Athens, I observe at
every turn that you are a most religious people" (see
Acts 17:22).

Each time I've been there I have sat and read the
words Paul spoke that day long ago, for what he said

then is as true today as it was then—and always has
been.

I've seen the giant Buddhas in Kamakura and
Nara, Japan, the beauty in the shrines of Kyoto and
Bangkok, the Hindu temples and the fervency at the
Ganges River in India, and the magnificent temple ruins
in Angor Wat in Cambodia. In each place I could have
said:

> Men of Japan, Thailand, India, Cambodia—wherever you
> are, whatever your country—I observe that you are a most
> religious people. Does God hear your prayers? If not, why
> not? If He does, then . . .

Jean Baptiste Lemoyne de Bienville, the French
explorer who founded New Orleans in 1718, said of the
Nez Perce Indians:

> Their honesty is immaculate and their purity of purpose
> and their observance of the rules of their religion are most
> uniform and remarkable. They are certainly more like
> saints than a horde of savages.[2]

In their history, the Jews had been exposed to the
religions of Egypt and of their neighbors—the Moa-
bites, Philistines, Edomites, Amorites, and others. Far
away in India the religion of Hinduism was on the scene
before Abraham, 1,200 years before Elijah. Perhaps
trade caravans had brought in some of Hinduism.

All of these were "a most religious people." But
what kind of a religion? The history of Israel has been
a repeated effort to get the people to affirm who is to be
their God. Shortly after the Exodus from Egypt, 500
years before Elijah, Joshua had confronted the people
with: "If you be unwilling to serve the Lord, choose this

day whom you will serve; . . . but as for me and my
house, we will serve the Lord" (Josh. 24:15).

And James Russell Lowell put it:

> Once to ev'ry man and nation
> comes the moment to decide,
> ....
> And the choice goes by forever.

There is a multiplicity of contemporary Baals from
which we could choose: nationalism, communism,
secularism, materialism, militarism, science, education,
social justice, human rights, ban the nukes, save the
whales, and the like. The danger in each is that their
ideals and institutions will shove God politely or impo-
litely aside.

The Christian task is not primarily to extend the
horizontal dimensions of wealth, property, social welfare, education, health, or to pour oil on the world's
machinery, or to think that if the world's machinery is
redesigned all will be well. All that may be a proper
Christian concern, but it is not the primary task. Our
task is vertical—to determine who is to be our God and
to establish a right relationship with God. There can be
no proper horizontal relationship unless the vertical is
in the proper place, and not always then.

Some years ago a volume was published which
summed up the major areas of that generation's life.
There were chapters about the arts and science, education, politics, economics, technological developments,
and the use of leisure time—recreation. There was no
chapter on religion. When the editor was questioned

about the omission, he said: "Well, no one of us thought he knew enough about religion to write about it."

That symposium's view of the world is clear—a secular civilization spreading around the world, with religion in general and Christianity in particular not playing a dominant role in it, but off in a compartment where people need not bother even to look at it.

In what I've read from the "futurists," those who write about what we can expect our future life to be like, there is relatively little about religion tomorrow. Even the best-seller, *Megatrends,* devotes little more than a page to religion, and most of that relates to what is happening now in terms of the TV-evangelists phenomenon.

But religion does play a vital role. The trouble in Northern Ireland has plenty to do with religion. The Ayatollah Khomeini overthrew the Shah of Iran in the name of religion, and his Islamic revolution is spreading into the Arab world. A large part of Lebanon's trouble is religious in nature, with the various sects of Islam, the Druse, and the Christians. And India is having religious problems with the Sikhs and Hindus. The United States is not at such a critical stage—yet. But these religions are infiltrating us and bringing their animosities with them. The way we Christians, even within the same family, fight each other is cause for sadness. Religion ought to be one of the most unifying forces in the world; instead, it can be one of the most divisive. When people are at their most religious peak, or "high," they can behave with the least sense and the severest cruelty.

Our generation is not irreligious, contrary to what some may think. The situation Joshua, Elijah, and Paul confronted faces us—only the form has changed. It is impossible to be irreligious. We human beings are incurably religious. We are a most religious people. Religion is what we practically believe in and give ourselves to. All of us are faced with an unavoidable choice: what kind of a religion will we choose? Who or what is to be our God?

To be religious is a part of our psychological make-up. We often use the word *faith* as a synonym for *religion!* and *religion* for *Christianity,* using the words interchangeably. In the broad sense we are right. What we put our faith in and give our devotion to becomes a religion for us. Faith is a capacity in human nature that we cannot be rid of. We exercise it all the time in some way or other, on something or other.

I'm a newspaper freak and read more than one daily. I read a regular column by a man who seems to consider himself irreligious. Whether he believes in God or not, I'm not sure, although there are occasional references to church. He seems to be for all religions equally, for all impress him as being equally unnecessary. His own pleasure and happiness, along with nature's beauty, are what he seems to care about. I suspect, though, that he has a residue of religious faith that he is unwilling to admit.

Everyone of us puts our faith in something, gives our devotion to something, for we are coerced by a psychological necessity to make a religion of something. You are religious, it says; you can never be irreligious. For your own sake, for the world's sake, face the question—what kind of a religion do you have? Who is your God?

Not only psychology, but history illustrates our religious nature, from primitive times to our own. Consider this example.

In central Greece near the Corinthian Gulf is a historic place called Delphi. The place was first settled by Minoan priests from Crete, who established a shrine to their deity around 1500 BC, 200 years before Israel's Exodus from Egypt. Sometime about 1,000 BC, the Greeks captured Delphi and founded the oracle of their god Apollo.

When Jesus was crucified, the Delphic shrine was older than Moses or Elijah, and older than the Roman Empire. Contrast the antiquity of Delphi and the might of the Roman Empire with the seeming feebleness of Jesus that day He was crucified on Calvary. We marvel that Rome fell, and Jesus has gone on to become the most influential spiritual force in the history of man. When Delphi, which represented a religion so ancient and seemingly permanent, began to dwindle, people could not believe their eyes. Two generations after Christ, Plutarch wrote that men had been "in anguish and fear lest Delphi should lose its glory of three thousand years." (Well, what was 1,500 years to Plutarch?) But Delphi faded out. It was not irreligion that caused the demise; another religion ended it, although to pit Jesus on Calvary against the antiquity, reverence, authority, and splendor of Delphi would at first seem foolish. The truth of history is that the only cure for religion is a better religion, never irreligion.

From the Delphis of the past to the galaxies of the future, there is religion. Literature, art, music, and philosophy all deal with religion; even science cannot

avoid it. In the movie *Space Odyssey: the Year 2001*
there was worship of that monolith, whatever it was.
Star Trek was good guys versus bad guys—Luke Sky-
walker and Darth Vader—good and evil.

I'm not a science-fiction buff, but from what I gather almost all of those writers deal with the good and evil
conflict, with the good triumphing. And that is religion.
C. S. Lewis, Madeleine L'Engle, and Ray Bradbury,
while subtle, are more specifically religious.

Whenever and wherever we talk about "values" we
are talking about religion, whether or not we call it that.

Today's world is not irreligious; it is very religious.
Religion is moving fast, vast, and potent these days. One
would be blind if the evidences of religion's power in the
structure, movement, and actions on today's world are
not seen. Were Paul here, he would say to us: "What
you worship in ignorance, I set forth to you" (Acts
17:23, author).

And Elijah would say: "Why do you vacillate between two alternatives?" (1 Kings 18:21, author).

This same truth confronts us in our churches. It is
easy enough to see why some people give up the church.
We talk a lot of antiquated nonsense at times. We speak
about some trivial, negative moralisms that flourish for
awhile and then fade away. Too many church members
give allegiance once a week, but do nothing during the
week. Churches themselves are caught up in how much
water is necessary for baptism, or what constitutes ordi-
nation and for whom, or who can partake of the Lord's
Supper and with whom. Religion, the church, ought to
be humanity's most unifying force. Instead, religion is

one of the world's most divisive forces. And that is
appalling.

When one of us criticizes religion, the church, let
us remember that what Jesus said about the religion of
His day was scathing. I wouldn't dare employ the brisk
vocabulary he used about the "organized church" of
His day: hypocrites, blind guides, whited sepulchers,
serpents, a generation of vipers. The gentle Jesus we
revere was saying that about the "church" then. But,
note this, he was not attacking the evils of religion with
irreligion, but in the name of a positive religion.

We are not irreligious; like the Athenians, we are
a most religious people. But what kind of a religion?
You have probably heard such statements as: "Too
many people have just enough religion to feel uncomfortable in doing wrong, but not enough to feel comfortable in doing right."[3]

I think E. Stanley Jones, early Methodist missionary, said that "too many of us have been innoculated
with a mild form of Christianity, just enough to make
us immune to the real thing."

To anyone who is resisting the church, I'm not
denying the validity of what you are saying. Jesus said
as much. But I do ask you to face up to what the
meaning of your rebellion is. Does it mean discomfort
in doing wrong? Does it mean immunity to the real
thing? Does it mean out of the church toward some kind
of a "feather-bed" religion? Or does it really mean an
apathy that doesn't really care? If it does, that will get
you nowhere. Going that way means only that there will
be a weaker form of religion.

It seems to me that the religion Jesus was trying to

get across had at least three elements. First, it was positive, not negative. The Judaism of Jesus' day was cluttered and bound with rules and regulations, most of which were some kind of a prohibition. Too much of today's Christianity stresses negatives, saying that a Christian is known for what he *does not* do, when it ought to be the other way around. Sure, Jesus said there was to be some denial—of this for that, but He emphasized the positive. Second, Jesus affirmed life. Today much in Christianity speaks in terms of life's sorrows, pain, and suffering. All that is a part of life. But to affirm life's goodness because God Himself is good is real Christianity. Third, Jesus, and especially Paul, talked about the joyous quality of life. *Rejoice* was one of Paul's favorite words. Of all people, Christians ought to be the most joyous, yet see how gloomy some Christians can be. Yes, Jesus was a man of sorrows, but He had the laughter of heaven in His eyes.

All of this is summed up in the ancient Shema:

Hear, O Israel, the Lord our God is one Lord; and you shall love the Lord your God with all your heart, and with all your soul, and with all your might (Deut. 6:4).

To which Jesus added, "You shall love your neighbor as yourself" (Matt. 22:39).

This is the primary confession of faith. It shows the uniqueness of God—Yahweh alone, the sole object of reverence and obedience. The phrase "You shall love the Lord your God" avoids an obedience based on necessity and duty. The way John put it, "We love because he first loved us" (1 John 4:19), is the root of that allegiance and obedience and is the practical basis of religion. No other religious faith offers such a profound insight. What such a religious faith requires is that we choose to accept it.

A bit earlier it was said that we often use the words *faith, religion,* and *Christianity* synonymously and interchangeably. But they are not really the same. They may relate, but each is distinct.

Alfred North Whitehead in *Religion in the Making* has a definition of religion:

> Religion is what the individual does with his own solitariness. It runs through three stages, if it evolves to its final satisfaction. It is the transition from God the void to God the enemy, and from God the enemy to God the companion.

That definition is not always popular among Christians. But Whitehead was defining *religion,* not Christianity. As such, religion can be a preparation for Christianity; religion is the effort—Christianity is the result. Perhaps we could say that primitive religion was the seeking religion; Judaism is the hoping religion. Christianity is the reality of what primitivism sought and Judaism hoped for. The distinction between Christianity and other religions is this—that in these others men are seeking after God, and Christianity is God seeking after men! And all that Christianity asks is, "Try it for yourself."

Two diverse personalities have given succinct comments on the distinction between religion and Christianity. The nineteenth-century Congregationalist, Henry Ward Beecher, said:

> Religion would frame a just man; Christ would make a

whole man. Religion would save a man; Christ would make him worth saving.

And in the twentieth century Anglican Archbishop William Temple said: "For the religious man to do wrong is to defy his King; for the Christian, it is to wound his Friend."

What does this distinction have to do with us in affirming who is to be our God? I'm speaking from the perspective of a Christian minister who wants you to decide on the God who revealed himself in Jesus Christ. In other words, choose the Christian way by choosing Jesus Christ.

There is a sentence attributed to an anonymous writer: "Christianity begins where religion ends—with the Resurrection."

And that is what Paul said to those "religious" Athenians, for he was preaching "Jesus and the resurrection." That gives Christianity a distinct difference. That difference bothered those Athenians, and it bothers some folk today. Being religious is one thing; being a Christian is another. Religion is the means for the end, and the end is God. In Jesus Christ God's grace showed us the way to affirm who is to be our God.

While I can see sincerity and morality in other religions, can appreciate and honor their prayers, and even find some appeal to some part of me in the serenity of Shinto, the quiet meditation of Buddha, the syncretism of the Hindu, the devotion of Islam, and especially Judaism's primacy of God; as with Elijah, there comes the point where there is to be no accommodation between the worship of any Baal or Yahweh.

> For Elijah, the co-existence, or the coalescence of the two
> forms of worship . . . was intolerable.[4]

We live in a world of many religions. I submit Jesus
Christ to you, not the Jesus of complicated doctrines
and trivial concerns, but Jesus Himself—the revelation
of the divine, the Savior of the human race. I ask you
to affirm who is to be your God by choosing Jesus Christ
and accepting God's grace. At our deepest level we
know that were we really to accept Him and be loyally
devoted to Him, then the world would truly be a better
place; it might even be saved.

5

One of God's Little Clouds
1 Kings 18:44

The fervent chant, "Run, Jesse, run! Run, Jesse, run!" heard so prominently in late 1983 and early 1984, would have had an entirely different connotation forty years earlier. Jesse would have been told to *run*, all right, but not for the presidency of the United States! That Jesse Jackson could seek the presidency is because of "a cloud no bigger than a man's hand."

After the fire had consumed the water-soaked altar on Mount Carmel, and before the rain came, Elijah commanded:

> Seize the prophets of Baal; let not one of them escape. And they seized them; and Elijah brought them down to the brook Kishon, and killed them there (1 Kings 18:40).

All 450 of them!

That mass massacre was not a pretty sight. In the name of religion we are horrified. But it was done in the name of religion. Certainly, religious people ought not to kill each other, we cry. But they did, and still do. It was a primitive, brutal time, almost as cruel as our own day.

The promised rain for which Elijah prayed had not

yet arrived. A servant was sent to look toward the sea
from which the autumnal rains came. The sky was
cloudless. Then he was told to go again, to go seven
times, to keep looking. "And at the seventh time he
said, 'Behold, a little cloud like a man's hand is rising
out of the sea' " (v. 44).

Then there was a torrential rain: "And Ahab told
Jezebel all that Elijah had done, and how he had slain
the prophets [of Baal] with the sword" (1 Kings 19:1).

Jezebel was furious! She sent Elijah a message,
warning him that within twenty-four hours he would
join those priests of Baal in death. So, before Elijah
could enjoy the triumph he fled in terror.

Perhaps there was more than fear of Jezebel. Perhaps there was an almost psychotic depression. He had
just presided over the brutal slaying of 450 men, and
with the sword at that. One cannot see that much
bloody death without experiencing severe depression.
Killing in war often does that. One of the aftermaths of
the Vietnam war was the deep emotional disturbances
caused by bestial killing. Despite our knowledge of the
human psyche, we still have not done so well in aiding
people to cope with their nightmares. In the next chapter we shall see more of how Elijah dealt with his fear
and depression.

Clouds are so delicate, lacy, and beautiful that they
play upon our fancies and stretch our imaginations. The
poet Wordsworth borrowed some 100-year-old lines
from fellow-poet John Milton:

> . . . lonely as a cloud
> That floats on high o'er vales and hills.

That cloud seen by the servant was different. It was lonely, but it would end the three and one-half year drought. It caused Mendelssohn to have the people in *Elijah* sing: "Thanks be to God! He laveth the thirsty land!" But clouds can also bring storms that disturb our tranquillity.

This chapter could look at a variety of small clouds of promise. However, I want to single out only one little cloud and trace how it broke a long period of drought.

The treatment of the American Negro is one of the dark blotches on our history. Perhaps only our treatment of the American Indian is worse. Too little has been done to rectify the Indian situation. Much has been accomplished in the area of black Americans. And this is the "little cloud" that I want to trace over a forty-year period.

Ideas, like life, never arrive full-grown; they must first be born, then nurtured, and allowed to mature. Sometimes an idea may be conceived and then aborted because it is too threatening. Sometimes an idea can become a mistress, and in the excitement and glamor one flirts back and forth in clandestine meetings, never making a commitment. Sometimes an idea and a person meet, and there is a kindred spirit relationship that develops into a meaningful and lasting association.

Once a person and an idea are committed the road is often rocky and dangerous. Perhaps it comes to the place where risk and danger threaten the commitment, and there is a separation, or even a divorce. Ideas are perpetuated just as life is, with the same traumas and happiness. It is often difficult to pinpoint an idea's conception. There is no calendar to locate the fertile period. Ideas may be latent or lie dormant. Then at the right time a person comes along to impregnate the seed-idea and bring it to life.

A latent seed-idea began to find some nourishment for me when I first met Shelton Bishop in the fall of 1943 at the Yale Divinity School. There could have been no more dissimilarity between two men. He was old enough to be my father. He was black, I was white. He was an urbane, sophisticated New Yorker; I was a plainsman from Oklahoma and West Texas. He was steeped in the Anglican tradition; I was a Southern Baptist, recently removed from the Pentecostals. I had never been associated with an Episcopal priest, nor had I personally known an educated Negro, the term then in use. "Black" did not come into use until twenty years later. He had never been in close association with a white Southerner. Racial prejudice was not a part of my youth. I think each of us fascinated the other. There was much we could learn from each other. Shelton and I began a relationship that ripened into a deep friendship which lasted until his death.

Father Shelton Bishop was rector of Saint Phillip's Church in New York City. Situated in the heart of Harlem, St. Phillip's was then celebrating its 125th anniversary. It was the largest and most prestigious Negro Episcopal church. Shelton Bishop was tall and bald. His nose was aquiline, sharp and hooked. He had thin lips, the bluest of blue eyes, and a skin complexion lighter than mine. He had less Negro blood than I have Indian blood.

I graduated from Yale in June 1944 and returned

to Baton Rouge. In December of that year Shelton proposed a visit. His son was a captain in the Army Air Corps, stationed in New Orleans. Shelton had never been South, and was coming to see his son. He would ride the bus to Baton Rouge.

It was wartime, and all transportation was crowded. The line waiting for the bus to Baton Rouge was long. In those days Negroes were the last to board and sat at the back of the bus. Sometimes they didn't get on at all. Shelton stood there in his clerical collar. A handsome man. The bus driver, thinking him to be a Catholic priest, invited: "Step right in, Father. Take this seat."

I met him at the bus station. Almost simultaneously with the greeting there was a poignant sob: "Avery, I didn't identify myself with my people."

I asked for an explanation. Remember, he'd never been in the South and was unaccustomed to the "Jim Crow" customs. He did not realize why he had been given a seat until about halfway on the trip. He had been mistaken for a white Roman Catholic priest and had been put on the bus while his fellow Negroes had been denied. The experience was shattering to him. Throughout the three-day visit he repeatedly returned to the refrain: "I didn't identify with my people."

Some ten years later I met Shelton in New York. We caught up on what had happened in the decade since we had last met. Then he returned to that day in 1944, and again that mournful refrain: "Avery, I didn't identify with my people." That was the last time I saw him. The words and the tone live on in me.

It is my belief that the church, churches, and

church people, white and black, have been and still are responsible for planting the seed of what we call the Civil Rights Movement. I hope that today's youth will hear from their churches that the church was and is responsible.

White and black churches and their members worked for what was called "better race relations." Each had to work within the framework of the societal structure of the day. They worked to effect change. They laid the groundwork for later achievements. When the time and climate were different, the system could be openly challenged. This is a fact that some of the current black leadership seems not to know or conveniently forgets. Black leaders now in their late sixties and seventies are called "Uncle Toms," and whites of the same age are looked upon as obstructionists. However, had it not been for those people in the 1940s-1950s, those of the 1960s and 1970s would have failed. Maybe there were some "Toms" among the blacks; that's the only way they could work. There was some paternalism among the whites; that's all they knew. But there was plenty of two-way understanding and mutual appreciation. What was accomplished may seen insignificant today, but those achievements were significant at the time. They were clouds no bigger than a man's hand.

The system within which I have worked for some forty-five years is the family of Christians known as Southern Baptists. Southern Baptists deserve some of the criticism they have had, but there is more that is favorable. For example, prior to the Civil War, Southern Baptists refused church office to slave holders. In

1908 the Convention adopted an antilynching resolution. Mob violence was deplored as early as 1928. Race relations as such was given repeated attention. The most far-reaching statement, called "A Charter of Christian and Baptist Principles and Their Necessary Consequences in Racial Attitudes," was adopted in 1947 and reaffirmed in 1948. To supplement the charter, "Some Principles of Conduct Resulting from These Beliefs" were also adopted in 1947 and reaffirmed in 1948. Let me list three of those principles to illustrate:

> We shall think of the Negro as a person and treat him accordingly.

> We shall protest against injustice and inequities against Negroes as we do in the case of people of our own race, whenever and wherever we meet them.

> We shall be willing for the Negro to enjoy the rights granted him under the Constitution of the United States, including the right to vote, to serve on juries, to receive justice in the courts, to be free from mob violence, to secure a just share of the benefits of educational and other funds, and to receive equal service for equal payment on public carriers and conveniences.

> (Southern Baptist Convention Annual for 1947-1948).

In 1947-48 that was radical! Then in 1954 the SBC affirmed the Supreme Court decision that declared school segregation to be unconstitutional.

White Baptists as a whole paid scant attention. There were too many "uncertain trumpets" in Baptist pulpits. However, there were some individuals and churches whose tones were certain. Some pastors were fired; some were censured; some were threatened. But most were not because the white conscience was troubled, and the Christian desire to do what was right was strong.

After the Supreme Court's desegregation decision I preached a sermon supporting that decision. The bank which had the church mortgage called in three of our deacons and threatened to foreclose that mortgage unless I kept quiet. Those deacons said: "We may not like what Avery Lee says. But neither this bank nor anyone else is going to tell him what he can or cannot preach." The Citizen's Council trotted out the unpolished rail to ride me out of town. They didn't. There was a letter from a white man in De Quincy, Louisiana:

> It was a privilege to be in your service on Sunday, April 8 . . . I have intended to ask you for a copy of the sermon you preached that morning (in which you) dealt with racial problems. I am glad that my son (a student at Louisiana Tech) has a man such as you for his pastor. /S/ Max Stracener.

Other pastors found similar support from their churches. But some were sent into the wilderness.

There were "little clouds" that seem as insignificant as the one spied by Elijah's servant.

One day in 1945 I went to the office of Dr. Gardner C. Taylor, pastor of the Mount Zion Baptist Church in Baton Rouge. What was significant about that? Nothing, from my point of view, although I am white and he is black. Years later, Gardner told his church in Brooklyn, New York, Concord Baptist, that I was the first white preacher ever to come to *his* office. To him, that was significant.

In Baton Rouge in 1940-42 I was director of the Baptist Student Union at Louisiana State University. Our student center was leased from the university. Dr. Felton Clark, president of Southern University (a state university for Negroes), and Dr. Martin Luther Harvey, Jr., dean of students at Southern, and I thought it would be a good idea for students of both campuses to meet together. I invited them to meet at our place, so I asked Major Frye, dean at Louisiana State University, if we could use the Baptist Student Center for an interracial student meeting. He replied: "Avery, don't ask me. If you ask, I will have to refuse; just go ahead and have the meeting."

We did. Sometimes when you ask, some "rule" must be invoked. If you go ahead, no one pays attention.

Again in Baton Rouge, I asked the Woman's Missionary Union president of the First Baptist Church if we could invite Dean Harvey to speak. She agreed, although to have a black man speak to a group of white ladies, unless he was an African "convert," simply wasn't done. The day he spoke happened to be the time when a fancy "tea" was planned. What to do about the black speaker? Georgia Williamson, beautiful, gracious, charming lady of the Old South, and the president, took care of that. She took him by the arm and led him to the head of the line. Don't ask questions; go ahead.

Pastors of Negro Baptist churches were, for the most part, not well-educated. A few were college graduates. Some had a high school diploma. White pastors would meet with a group of black pastors. Basic courses in the Bible, elementary sermon preparation, Sunday School organization, and church administration would be taught. So elementary now, so fundamental then. In New Orleans the Union Baptist Theological Seminary was begun in 1937. All the officers were black, the teachers were white; faculty and graduate students were from the New Orleans Baptist Theological Seminary. The school was never accredited, but the teaching was good.

We had interracial worship services, especially on Brotherhood Sunday. Even worshiping together was an achievement. We could go to their churches, but they couldn't come to ours, unless invited.

We whites could and did support better education for blacks. The "separate-but-equal" doctrine of the time was only half-true. When J. K. Haynes, executive secretary of the Louisiana Teachers Association (black teachers), pleaded for equal pay, whites supported him. He succeeded in 1947 with persuasion and an appeal to economic fairness.

Ralph Jones began his career as an educator in 1926 with the Louisiana Negro Normal and Industrial Institute. There were a few frame buildings, seventeen faculty members, and 120 students. That institute became Grambling State University, with Ralph Jones as president for forty years. Grambling developed an international reputation, with a multi-million dollar campus, a faculty and staff of six hundred, and over four thousand students. Of course, the human relations climate changed in those years. Younger blacks of the civil rights era called Ralph Jones an "Uncle Tom." He did not deserve that. He was not that. He was a wily manipulator of the system who worked within the framework of reality. He could not demand; he asked.

What appeared as groveling was in reality seeing some "hand-sized clouds become reality." Call it "benevolent paternalism," if you will, but he could not have succeeded without the support of whites who believed in the same causes.

When the integration of schools came to New Orleans in 1960, a gallant white Methodist pastor and Rabbi Julian Feibleman walked to school with a frightened black grammar-school child and her parents. Ironically, the black family name was "Christian."

Those "little clouds" in Louisiana, Mississippi, and other Southern states, and even in some Northern states, got together and rain laved the dry, thirsty land. And, yes, there were storms, violent at times, with floodwaters and hurricane winds. Some things were destroyed; some good things along with the bad were washed away. And there were some gentle rains which soaked down deep and restored the water tables of decency. Both kinds were needed. The destruction caused by the storms brings pain and suffering. But there is the opportunity to restore or create something new. The new may not have the same beauty or sentiment of the old, but in time the new will mature, age, and have an "antique" beauty and sentiment of its own.

Were I black, I might want more torrential rains to wash away all the debris that has piled up and prevented me from having what I deserve. But, as a white man, I deplore much of what I see. My Depression-Protestant-work-ethic background rebels at "entitlement demands." No one is *entitled* to anything, other than equal opportunity and a responsible use of those opportunities.

I could give some results of what these "clouds" have produced, but you are aware of and know them. Since I've been talking about the church, churches, and church members, let me close with one significant illustration of what has happened within the Southern Baptist family of Christians.

(In 1983) . . . there are approximately 300,000 black members in an estimated 3,750 churches. (In 1944 there were none!) Approximately 750 congregations are predominately black and have about 250,000 members. . . Nearly 100 black professionals are employed by Southern Baptist agencies. . . . There is no way accurately to count how many black Southern Baptists there are because membership by race is not reported by the churches.[1]

"Thanks be to God! He laveth the thirsty land!" And Jesse can run, not walk!

6

When the Bottom Drops Out, God Confirms Himself
1 Kings 19:1-18

It is difficult to imagine a more dramatic shift in tone and mood from that of Elijah's victory over the priests of Baal and Elijah's fleeing in terror. Although there is no biblical explanation, there is a human explanation. Elijah was going through what all idealists experience when they discover that there are no permanent victories over evil. It seemed to Elijah that the Lord had let him down by leading him into a crisis and then deserting him.

Depressed and frightened, he fled into the wilderness, a situation we have all faced. The fleeing Elijah was in need of some beliefs to strengthen him—belief in himself, in his cause, and in his God, or perhaps in the reverse order. He may have been free for the time from Ahab and Jezebel, but he was a prisoner of himself. Both his heart and his mind had gone into hiding along with his body. When doors are slammed shut against us, we are prone to draw into ourselves and lock others out. Distrust begets distrust—then comes self-pity. Fretted by the injustice inflicted upon him, Elijah lost his judgment and compassion, and vowed vengeance.

Heine, the poet, was only half in jest when he wrote:

> My wishes are a humble dwelling with a thatched roof, a good bed, good food, flowers at my windows, and some fine trees before my door. And if the good God wants to make me completely happy he will grant me the joy of seeing six or seven of my enemies hanging from the trees.

We are looking at this episode from the perspective of some thirty centuries, and we can see a purpose, a similar purpose, which we may need to see in our own lives. God was to reveal himself in rational human experience rather than in the supernatural event of Mount Carmel. Although it is true that God can and does reveal Himself in other ways than the spectacular, this is not the main point of the story. Rather, the message is clear in the use of repetition: "What are you doing here, Elijah?"

And the prophet answered: "The people of Israel have forsaken thy covenant . . . and I . . . only am left" (1 Kings 19:9-10, 13-14).

In the Mount Carmel episode Elijah's being alone was interpreted in the positive manner of an exhilarating conflict; here his aloneness had the opposite effect—he felt sorry for himself and wanted to die. God's response to that was a stern rebuke: "I have seven thousand others left!" (1 Kings 19:18, author).

Elijah was not indispensable, nor are we; there are always others. But God still had a task for Elijah which only he could do.

So the story in chapter 19 has a major effect on how we understand the conflict on Mount Carmel. Even

Elijah misunderstood its significance and expected God to continue the spectacular. The events after the contest shifted to something more vital. Chapter 18 deals with the issues of national apostasy, whereas chapter 19 focuses on individual faith. Chapter 18 portrays the outer battle of faith, while 19 deals with the inner struggle for faith.

The two stories make different points and set forth the convex and concave sides of what the Bible means by faith. Together they reflect the tensions between the public and the private struggle between faith and unbelief. Together the two stories constitute a single biblical testimony regarding God's call to obedient service. We need the whole story, not just its separate parts, to grasp the full reality.

The war of nerves has always gone on in human experience, and obviously a person who does not win that war cannot win anything else. Today, however, not only are our private tensions and strains a part of us, but the newspapers and TV storm our minds with the perils and afflictions of all humanity: refugees, war, terrorism, poverty, starvation. Our own country is divided in mind and attitude, precarious in its situation, frustrated even with all its power and held captive by "a mouse that roars." It would be easy for us to cry with Elijah, "It is enough!"

In such a time our Christian faith ought to count, if it is any good at all. If our Christian faith can't help, then it must be a shallow and conventional affair, and we might as well look for something else.

To suppose that a dangerous situation must issue in self-pity, fearfulness, and panic is to misread human nature *and God!* Peril pulls the trigger, but what explodes depends upon what we're loaded with. One collapses in frightened weakness, and another responds with released energies. And the second response can come out of the first. So, let's start by getting over the idea that a dangerous situation is necessarily lamentable. It is not! Peril is one of the major stimulants in human history, and out of dangerous situations the finest things in life have come.

Scientific medicine, for example, was born in fear. From yellow fever to polio to cancer, we face dangerous enemies that we are rightfully afraid of, and that fact has proved to be the strong sentiment that has moved us to amazing achievements. Some fears have been conquered, some are "on the ropes," and others are still being probed.

If we are to meet these current perils, we must do something practical, *act!* Stop sitting around; go out and do something. Advises one psychiatrist: "The most drastic and usually the most effective remedy for fear is direct action." We should be thankful that we do not have to live through days like these without an undergirding faith that God is not dead, and we are His only ones left—not even we 14 million Southern Baptists, though we often act as if we are!

I found a simple outline for a sermon based on this episode in Elijah's life. I'm going to give it to you, but not develop it here. It will fit generally into what I will write later.

1. Get Up—"Arise and eat" (19:5). The body has a part to play. You never know what you can do until you try. Too many of us never try until we know what

we can do. Some physical action, some duty near at hand, and within the present range of possibility, starts the restoration of confidence, even while the mist of despair engulfs us.

2. Look Up—"Go forth, and stand on the mount before the Lord" (v. 11). As the body, so must the mind and spirit be fed.

3. Link Up—"Go, return on your way" (v. 15). New work and new companions were to be found in Damascus. So find the enlargement that comes from widened interests. In self-forgetting service, comforting and encouraging others, Elijah would find himself and his purpose.

This Elijah episode is our story, too, although perhaps not in such dramatic form. The threat, real or imagined; the flight of terror into some wilderness of despair; the wonder of being sustained; the darkness, stillness, and the strangely comforting loneliness of a cave in which we spend whatever time is required for the noise and fury of our personal hell to subside; the perception of the gift of a gentle silence, then the miracle of discovering again the reality (the *is*ness) of God; our protest against not being allowed to stay in whatever serene haven of rest we have found, but being sent back out to face life and people—all this mirrors our life experiences. The whole kaleidoscopic experience is real, weaker in some, stronger in others.

Now I want to retrace Elijah, drawing heavily upon the insights of Dr. B. Davie Napier, a contemporary of mine at Yale, and an outstanding Old Testament scholar. Dr. Napier translates Jezebel's message as it is preserved in the Septuagint, the Greek translation of the

Hebrew Old Testament in the closing years of the pre-Christian era: "If you are Elijah, then I am Jezebel." Then he interprets the sentence this way: "You may be a prophet, but I am royalty; your name may mean 'God is Yahweh,' but as long as I am here neither you nor Yahweh will stand in the kingdom of this royal house."[1]

Let me put this in the context of a personal situation of thirty years ago. I had preached a sermon on integration. A group said: "If you are Avery, we are the Citizens Council. We will get the bank to foreclose the church mortgage and run you out of town." So Avery was almost ready for a trip to the cave. You see, there are varieties of traumas to send us running, as it were, to some cave in the desert.

This Elijah of the Old Testament was terrified, scared out of his wits, and running for his life. He was prudently aware of Jezebel's implicit threat, for he knew she had done it before and would do it again. His fear makes him more human and brings him closer to us. These biblical heroes were people like us, very human. Being a follower of God, doing what we feel is God's will, does not provide us with immunity from risk, free us from doubt, or make us fearless. Our life of Christian service, like Elijah's, is enhanced by our acknowledgement of our full susceptibility to all the natural shocks that flesh and faith are heir to.

Some scholars have suggested that Elijah was suicidal. Well, maybe there is a bit of that, even as that time when Moses cried: "If this is the way it is to be, then take my life" (Num. 11:15, author).

Elijah was devastated, in despair, and shattered—and this was soon after his resounding triumph on

Mount Carmel. He was a forerunner of many of us, especially preachers who, when things are rough, moan:

> God, you can have the whole thing! I've had it! I've had all I can stand! Get her off my back! And if you can't do that, then this whole thing stinks, and I want out! I'm no better than my ancestors, those who've gone before me. It is enough! Take my life, since, God knows, I'm no better than they."[2]

Then, exhausted, he went to sleep. Someone touched him and instructed, "Wake up and eat." And there was bread and water, so he ate and took off for Horeb. And, here we go again—more improbable ravens and another drying stream. Who was this "someone"? Who called? When someone, anyone, helps us we are thankful. It is a fact of faith that sustenance comes in ways that are incredible, even in our flights of terror through the wilderness of despair.

So, "coming to the cave, he spent the night." Here we have a scene very much like that of Moses on Mount Sinai (Horeb) where there were peals of thunder, flashes of lightning, dense clouds of smoke, and loud trumpet blasts. Note the similarity in the Elijah sequence:

> There was a mighty wind; God was not in the wind. And after the wind, an earthquake; God was not in the earthquake. And after the earthquake, fire; and God was not in the fire. And after the fire . . . *a sound of gentle silence*" (1 Kings 19:11-12, Napier).

When the deafening sound of the awful violence of nature is past, there is that sudden, contrasting gentleness of quiet, that audible "voice of silence"—God speaking. That "still small voice."

In this year of our Lord, we have had volcanic eruptions, earthquakes, tornados, floods, and hurricanes. As usual, there has been a revival of "we are living in the last days," and some with an eye on the profits from a best-seller, try to scare us into belief. *I don't believe that!* We've heard it all before, for centuries. Anyway, I question why make all that money if the end is so near that you can never use it. And you sure can't take it with you! If I'm wrong and they turn out to be right, at least none of them will be around to say, "I told you so." More important, for Moses, Elijah, and us? God *was not* speaking in the loud voice of nature's violence.

Impressed with hearing God in the "sound of gentle silence," Elijah went outside the cave and heard God ask: "Elijah, what are you doing here?" Now watch the defense mechanism, the rational justification, come into play. Again, so like us. What kind of a God is this? Doesn't He understand that it's because of being His prophet that I am here in this cave, shattered, exhausted, emotionally drained, running, and hiding to save my life? I don't need this criticism; I need the healing comforting, affirming, stroking word.

> I'm here because I'm devoted to You and served You well, even while the people deserted You. Your altars have been destroyed, Your prophets have been put to death. I'm the only one left, and Jezebel is after me. And You ask why I'm here? (vv. 10, 14, author).

Then God spoke:

> Go back the way you have come. . . . Retrace your steps; return to where and what you were because there are still

seven thousand left in Israel whose knees have never bent to Baal, nor whose lips have kissed him" (vv. 15-18, author).

Why have we become a generation of frightened cave-seekers? Well, if Elijah is legion, so is Jezebel; and if Jezebel is legion, so are the caves.

The flight to the caves is undertaken by vast numbers of people for a vast variety of reasons, and the nature of the caves varies.

The expressway to the caves is a traffic jam embracing us all: rich and poor, royalty and commoner, black and white, free and slave, educated and illiterate, male and female, owner and laborer, exploiter and exploited—all of us bent on escaping from what we think to be an unremedial, intolerable situation—all of us seeking a modicum of peace. And the range of the caves runs from the old standbys of sex, alcohol, and drugs to all the "T"s:

TA— Transactional Analysis
TM—Transcendental Meditation
TV— Television
TF— Touchy-feely group encounters
TZ— Try Zen and even in some circles as a last resort,
TJ— Try Jesus.[3]

But there is one more 'T' in the series: *Turn back* to where and what you were, because there are 7,000 (70 × 7,000!) others, and we need each other.

Some caves may be essential at times—*if we find God there!* For then we can leave the cave with our fear and terror, if not allayed, at least under control; with new resources given us to face the unanswerable questions with courage and strength; with disillusionment transformed into fresh determination; with contempt for society converted again to compassion and resolution; and with despair turning once more to prophetic passion.

The cave may be good, recreative, and therefore essential; *but not cavism*—that would institutionalize the cave, and we don't need that. The cave gives shelter when the furies without and within are raging out of control. But when the "gentle sound of silence" comes, then God assures us that we are not alone, that we are surrounded by a "cloud of witnesses," that there is work to be done and colleagues with whom we are to work. And, always, along the way, find, enlist, inspire some Elisha to take our place. We may go to the cave when we must, when, in whatever way, we hear: "If you are Elijah, I am Jezebel." But our lodging is to be only temporary.

In the apple orchard section of Maine there was an apple tree so loaded with fruit that, all around, the laden branches were propped up to keep them from the ground. A visitor exclaimed about the abundant crop. The owner of the orchard said: "Go back and look at that tree's trunk near the bottom." There the visitor saw that the tree had been badly wounded with a deep gash. Remarked the owner:

> That is something we have learned about apple trees. When the tree tends to run to wood and leaves and not fruit, we wound it, gash it, and almost always, no one knows why, this is the result: It turns its energies to fruit.

The late Edward R. Murrow, famous World War II correspondent, wrote of an experience he had:

> In the autumn of 1940 when the British stood alone, when the bombers came at dusk each evening and went away at dawn, I observed a sign on a church just off the East India Dock Road; it was crudely lettered and it read, IF YOUR KNEES KNOCK, KNEEL ON THEM.

Heavenly Father, our knees knock often; so here we are to kneel on them and listen for Your quiet voice to speak words of confirmation that will get us out of our "blue-funk" moods. From whatever cave we are in, we would get up, look up, and link up our lives with You by faith in Jesus Christ.

7

God Always Leaves
a Remnant
1 Kings 19:9-18; John 1:4

You may remember an early TV show about the harrowing experiences of a private investigator called "The Outsider." Each episode began with a segment which landed David Ross (Darren McGavin) into such a complicated predicament that it seemed impossible for him to get out of the mess. Then, as the camera would hold a "stop action" on the scene, Mr. Ross would comment: "You may be wondering how I got into a situation like this." And, whether or not we were wondering, for the next hour (between commercials) we were told how he got in and how he got out.

Thirty centuries ago a man named Elijah sat alone in a cave wondering how he had gotten into such a life-threatening situation. He had successfully confronted the priests of Baal on Mount Carmel, and a three and one-half year drought had ended. Then Queen Jezebel went after him with a vengeance. A disspirited Elijah cried: "It is enough; now, O Lord, take away my life; for I am not better than my fathers. . . . I, even I only, am left; and they seek my life to take it away.

Then God confronted Elijah in the episode of a

dreadful storm of combined wind, earthquake, and fire, but God spoke in a quiet voice:

> Go, return on your way to Damascus; and when you arrive, you shall anoint . . . Elisha . . . to be prophet in your place. . . . I will leave seven thousand in Israel, all the knees that were not bowed to Baal, and every mouth that has not kissed him (1 Kings 19:15-16, 18).

In other words, no matter how desperate the situation, none of us is the only one. God always has a remnant of the faithful. Throughout the Old and New Testaments, and in subsequent history, there is the theme, repeated as in a jubilant symphony: "I will keep a remnant."

There sat Elijah, feeling he was the only one left who believed in and was loyal to God. And there was God saying there are 7,000 others. And here we are, wondering whom to believe.

Such personal frustration is a major ordeal we face today. We look at the world and see convulsions everywhere: Northern Ireland, Lebanon, India, Central America, Africa—and so much of the trouble is caused by religion. The situation involves such ominous catastrophes as to make the ablest statesmen—presidents, prime ministers, and kings, for all their prime-time TV speeches—quake in their boots.

Then we look at ourselves, one by one. What can we do? What can we individually do? The scope of it is so vast, the factors determining what will come of it so far beyond our individual control, that as we face it we feel futility and helplessness. To be sure, we go on, trying to do our little bit here and there. But we do wonder what kind of a world will come of it for our children.

What the Irish Republican Army or the Iranians or the Russians or the Israelis or our President decide may shape humanity's destiny. But what can you or I do about any of that? Probably nothing. Perhaps a little.

In the long run everything good or bad depends upon individuals. These global wars cause us to send our young men. International business would bog down were it not for us. If individuals count for so much in war or business, why can't they count in international good-will and world peace? If hope for something better goes out of the lives of ordinary people, then it is all over for social and political civilization. Therefore, never let us forget the impact of the few. The heroes of life in this world have been the few. There is not a social, political, or religious privilege that has not come from the hard, sacrificial, and patient suffering of some minority which has stood steadfast in moral conflict and achieved all that is noble in the history of man.

We read that the ancient Greeks sentenced Socrates to death. There were 501 men on the jury that condemned Socrates: 281 of them voted for his death, 220 for his acquittal. If only 61 had changed their vote! Think of the crucial 5-4 decisions of our Supreme Court where one vote determined "the law of the land." The most prolific and edible grains mankind depends upon today are varieties that come from Marquis wheat and its hybrids. Millions of tons are produced in America and used to help feed the world (in 1907 there were only twenty-three pounds of Marquis wheat in the world). When that day a multitude was hungry and a lad came forth with a lunch of five loaves of bread and two fish, Andrew asked: "What are they among so many?" (John 5:9) That was not the last word; it is the first word in a world where God still works.

I've long had an interest in the biblical "doctrine of the remnant." Remnant is a "code word" for Jewish dispersal throughout the world. But it is more than that. The remnant is the depository of spiritual values to be carried on. It is God who leaves the remnant, and it is the evidence of God's grace. Much is made of the remnant in the Old Testament long before Elijah.

There was Noah. There was Abraham. There were Joseph and his brothers. There was Moses, the only male Hebrew child whose life was spared at that time. There was the Exodus from Egypt, then Elijah, then the Babylonian Exile and the return. Finally, in the New Testament there were Jesus, Paul, the twelve disciples, and the church. Now here we are.

For 2,000 years the history of the Christian church has been that of birth, life, death, and resurrection, always a remnant. The remnant is both individual and collective. It is both idea and historical fact. In the Old Testament the remnant was a dwindling that would revive. In the New Testament its destiny was to expand.

Look at China. In 1950 all Christian missionaries were expelled, and the churches were closed. I was in China in 1979. No churches were open. Two years later some were open, and more are open today. There is no full religious freedom. But there were those 7,000 who did not bow the knee to Mao Tse-tung. One cannot say that God has forsaken His people so long as there is a remnant in the church.

Disspirited and apparently defeated, Elijah was convinced that he was the only one left. Actually, he was one among many. Elijah is the classic example of a pessimism predicated on judgments based on appearances. Even when the outlook is bleak enough to justify despair, there are signs, for those who will see and recognize them, of an unfailing purpose. Pique and self-importance are factors which prompt us to exaggerate our own importance. Long ago Sophocles said:

> I beg you, do not be unchangeable. Do not believe that you alone can be right. The man who thinks that, the man who maintains that only he has the power to reason correctly, the gift to speak the soul—a man like that, when you know him, turns out empty.

Along with the doctrine of the remnant, we see Elijah facing the problem of the plateau: what to do when we reach some goal and then have to face weariness; what to do when the excitement becomes monotony; how to face ennui? This can and does happen to a person and to any institution, even a church. It is the the challenge, planning, and doing that create excitement. Achievement becomes a prelude to boredom. No, I can't say that Elijah was bored, but he was depressed. His achievement had not brought the acclaim that he expected.

To phrase it another way, what was he to do now? How do you replace a lost dream? Well, first remember that no dream is ever lost except through achievement. As Khalil Gibran put it: "To realize a dream is to kill it."

When a dream is realized it is time to have another dream.

H. T. Carruth put it: "There's nothing much to do but bury a man when the last of his dreams is dead."

Was that Elijah—his dream of defeating Baal achieved, sitting on the plateau of depression, needing a new dream? In some ways, yes.

Some years ago in Maine a little town named Flagstaff was to be flooded to become part of a large lake for which a dam was being built. All repairs and improvements in the town stopped. Why paint a house? Why repair anything? Everything was to be destroyed anyway. So, week after week, the town deteriorated. One man, later telling of the experience, gave this explanation: "Where there is no faith in the future there is no power in the present."

What a profound word! Of course the people of Flagstaff had no faith in their future and thus no power for their present—not until they had a dream of a future someplace else. Elijah was right in his depressed darkness, but he was wrong in thinking he was the only one who believed in God. He needed to be reminded that there were at least 7,000 others, and that meant a future. We need to be reminded that the church will never be left without power and direction. As Vachel Lindsay wrote:

> What is the final ending?
> The issue, can we know?
> Will Christ outlive Mohammed?
> Will Kali's altar go?
> This is our faith tremendous,—
> Our wild hope, who shall scorn—

That in the name of Jesus
The world shall be reborn![1]

Dark nights of the spirit come to everyone of us, maybe not with the same intensity as Elijah or the resignation of Flagstaff, but they come. They come not only to individuals but also to us collectively. Darkness has become symbolic of trouble and evil. The remnant which waits on the plateau yearns for light, not a floodlight, just a wee, penetrating beam.

Can you recall how the New Testament pictures the birth of Jesus? The emphasis is on the fact that *it was at night,* during the darkness.

> Shepherds keeping watch over their flocks by night,
> Wise Men following the star through the night.
> Herod in a midnight council decreeing the slaughter of innocent children.

Against such encompassing darkness, *Jesus came as light.*

We say that this is a dark time in the world, not the first and probably not the last. This is indeed a midnight time. Prophets of doom, especially some Christian preachers, seem to take a morbid delight in proclaiming that "it is two minutes till midnight." But let us not forget that Jesus was born into a similarly dark world. Eighteen centuries later, Phillips Brooks wrote of Bethlehem:

> Yet in thy dark streets shineth
> The everlasting light.

The world's darkness is all the more reason for us to

understand what faith in God and belief in Jesus Christ really mean.

Almost one hundred years after Bethlehem, the writer of the Fourth Gospel thought of Jesus in terms of light shining in the darkness. John was living in Ephesus. It was a time shadowed by violence. Yet something happened to him that changed sunset to sunrise. All through his Gospel John speaks of Jesus in terms of *life* and *light.* In the first chapter he says: "In him was life, and the life was the light of men. The light shines in the darkness, and the darkness has not overcome it" (John 1:4-5). Or, as J. B. Phillips translates it: "The light still shines in the darkness, and the darkness has never put it out."[2]

William Barclay states that the two basic words of John's Gospel are *life* and *light.* John begins (1:4) and ends (20:3) with life and light. The word life is used thirty-five times and the verb "to live" fifteen times. Light is used twenty-one times.[3] When Jesus enters a life, light comes, and the light Jesus ushers in puts darkness to flight. Darkness is hostile to light, but however hard the darkness tries, it cannot extinguish the light. The darkness (evil) may hate God and Christ, but it cannot put out either of them. Darkness can never understand, overcome, or extinguish the light.

Although Jezebel did all she could to obscure God's light, she failed. Although men do all they can to extinguish Christianity, they fail. In every generation Jews have and still talk about God. The light of Jesus Christ shines in all the world.

At first the radiance of Jesus was so limited. John stands in awe before the fact that after nearly a century that light is still shining—and brighter. Here we are twenty centuries later, seeing and knowing that the light is in the whole world, outnumbered to be sure, but the largest single religious light in the world, still shining, though shaded in some places, for it has never been put out.

My soul! What would Elijah say? How would he feel? Not 7,000 others, but nearly thirteen million Jews loyal to his God and almost one billion Christians loyal to his God's Son. Why, that's nearly one-third of the world's population. I can imagine a soft smile on the old prophet's face and a tear trickling down his creased cheek.

Elijah saw only the darkness. We are tempted to be obsessed with the darkness. This is a gloomy time, we complain. John took the darkness for granted. Of course, darkness. What kind of a world do you think this is? Quit kidding yourselves with sentimental optimism. Face up to reality. The sin of the world is ghastly. The dilemma of the world is desperate. Man's moral evil is profound. Yes, John took the world's midnight for granted, but he didn't stop there. With amazement and gratitude he saw the light, and emphasized *that. There* to him was the astonishing fact—that against the world's dark night a guiding star had shone, into that gloom a flaring hope had come, and all the hosts of evil are unable to put it out.

Here are three lessons for us:

1. There is God Who through Jesus Christ consummated the victory of light over darkness.
2. There is the heritage of God's continuing influence

to which we should give our personal faith and allegiance.

3. There is the assurance this truth brings.

The affirmation of the remnant idea, the plateau, or the light is set forth in the first words of Genesis: "In the beginning God created the heavens and the earth" (1:1).

Rather than looking at Genesis as an explanation of the origin of the universe, let's see it as an expression of faith, trust, and confidence in God. The account is the medium used to express this faith. The message is not creation; *it is the faith that God is God, a God who can be trusted because all times, things, places, events, and people are in His hands.*

The musical play *Camelot* is the story of King Arthur and the idealism of the knights of the Round Table. It was an idyllic place with a high quality of idealism and trust. Then that kingdom began to come apart at the seams, shattered from within. Queen Guinevere and Sir Lancelot betrayed the trust with their illicit affair, and the machinations of Mordred sowed the seed of disintegration. Finally a war brought it all down. Excalibur was returned to the lake.

There is a poignant scene near the end of the show. The war has left the Round Table in shambles and Camelot in disarray. Arthur is sitting alone pondering how, when, and why it all went wrong. A lad comes along and says that he wants to be a knight of the Round Table. He and Arthur talk about Camelot. The boy asks how to get there. Arthur points in that direction and says: "Run, boy, run!" The Camelot dream

never dies; always someone will come along to revive it
and keep it alive. Violent, destructive, greedy, and falli-
ble as he may be, man retains his vision and resumes his
search. "I will keep a remnant. . . . I will leave seven
thousand in Israel. . . . The light still shines in the
darkness, and the darkness has never put it out."

8

The Surprising God Who Goes in Advance

1 Kings 19:15-18; 2 Kings 2:1-15; Psalm 21:3

The picture the psalmist gives us in Psalm 21:3: "For thou dost meet him with goodly blessings," is that of a God *who is always ahead of us.* A more accurate reading would go: *"Thou goest ahead of him* with the blessings of goodness." The provisions of this God are always in advance. God answers sooner than we expect, sometimes before we ask. This is the picture of a God who springs surprises upon us, not only by coming to meet us, but by going in advance of us. The picture is enlarged in the 139th Psalm which tells us that anywhere we go, God is already there. We can neither get away from nor go ahead of God.

Ray Bradbury has a short story where a spacecraft lands on a planet which has a totally peaceful existence. The reason for the peace, they explain, is "the man is here" or "the man has been here." One of the crew members decides to stay. The captain decides to try and find "the man" on some other planet, but he is always a bit late. He searches for, but never finds "the man."

This is an attribute of God which we have not only neglected, but seemingly have forgotten altogether. The

sovereignty of God is one of the most needed emphases
of our day.

We don't know if Elijah knew this psalm or not. He
might have, because it was written years earlier. At any
rate, Elijah needed its truth. There he sat in his cave,
moaning that he was the only one left who believed in
God. Then God commanded: "Go, return on your way
to the wilderness of Damascus; and when you arrive
you shall anoint . . . Elisha . . . to be prophet in your
place" (I Kings 19:15-16).

God always has someone ready to take our place
and continue His work.

There are Christians today, generally sincere and
zealous, who are fond of organizing massive rallies to
give testimony to their faith. Such testimonies are basi-
cally all right. But I've seen too many that are little
more than organized, calculated, self-conscious parad-
ing of what ought to be something personally sacred.
When we Baptists have such a meeting we seem to be
testifying to convince our fellow Baptists we are more
Baptistic than they are.

Another emphasis in such a meeting is that of
answered prayer. People ask God for things, and God
unfailingly gives. And sometimes God is asked for some
remarkable, even trivial things. There is certainly nothing wrong with this. It is well in order to testify to
answered prayer. We don't do enough of that. But how
often do we hear anything about an "unanswered"
prayer? The psalmist declares in the opening words of
the twenty-first Psalm: "Thou hast given him his heart's
desire, and hast not withheld the request of his lips."

The psalmist was not as reluctant as we are in

acknowledging the goodness of God. God is good, he sang, not because He has given what was requested, but because He has given what *was not* asked for. God goes ahead of us. He anticipates our needs and comes to meet us with ample provisions. He surprises us in advance.

A. J. Gossip, a famous Scottish preacher of the early twentieth century, tells of hearing a man preach on the text: "Ask and it shall be given you" (Matt. 7:7, KJV). The preacher began by saying that God never gives unless we ask. This was an assertion, said Gossip, " . . . so entirely, obviously, and incredibly untrue that I never recovered."

God never gives unless we ask? Why, 90 percent of what God showers upon us are blessings for which we have never asked. We never went running after God for the primary resources which make life what it is. God came to meet us with what He had already done in advance.

In the first portion of this chapter, let me remind us of some of the surprises, some of the blessings with which God has met us in advance. In the second portion we shall look at what we can expect.

Ignatius Loyola, founder of the Jesuits, sat down one day to make an inventory of the gifts God had given him for which he had never asked. He never proceeded beyond the first item—myself! There he sat for hours staring at this one word: "I am a gift of God to me for which I never asked."

Perhaps every child has asked, and every parent remembers the child coming to ask: "Why am I *me?*" Whenever we ask that question, either in childish naïveté or in adult sophistication, we become philosophers, puzzling over the meaning of existence and our place in it.

Maybe this is a bit abstruse for some of us. So look at something a little closer to home. If ours were the right kind of a home, the advance gift to us was a home where preparation was made for our birth, to care for our every need.

> Before our eyes could focus or our hands could hold on, or before we could utter a cry, provision was made for us.
>
> Before we could feel cold we were wrapped in warm clothing.
>
> Before we could say we were hungry, there was mother's milk or a bottle of formula.

You see, many of us came into a whole circle of advance planning because there was caring love.

Someone may remark that this is mere preacher talk, that this is the love and care of parents and has nothing to do with God.

Beginning before Eden, God made the same kind of provisions for His people. In Eden was everything Adam and Eve needed, *before* they were even created. And had not God provided for Elijah on earlier occasions, albeit the provisions were on the sparse side? If we take the Christian view of life as taught by Jesus, that God is the Heavenly Father, then the right kind of parental love is seen as an echo of the love of that Heavenly Father.

The same thought is true about the experience of salvation. Here, too, God surprises us in advance. Salvation is nothing *we do.* Even when we respond to the call for repentance, it is because God has already taken

the initiative in Jesus Christ. Often at baptismal services we sing: "O happy day that fixed *my* choice On
Thee . . ." as if we do the choosing and God is the object
of our choice. To an extent that is true. But read again
the story of the conversion of Saul of Tarsus, who also
was on the road to Damascus. Can you imagine Paul,
looking back on the strange events on that road, sing-
ing: "O happy day that fixed my choice"? Not at all! He
didn't know what happened. He had not chosen Jesus;
Christ had chosen him! What transpired bewildered him
to the end of his days: "Unto me, who am less than the
least of all saints, is this grace given" (Eph. 3:8, KJV),
he testified.

You see, we don't have to run after God. He comes
running to us. In this greatest of all gifts God surprises
us in advance. God takes the initiative.

If this is true about the home into which we were
born, and the salvation we experience, it is also so of the
church in which we find fellowship. It is true that many
folk merely find themselves within the warmth of the
church's fellowship because their parents are there.
Children do deserve to have a church home bequeathed
to them by Christian parents before they ever ask. And,
remember, Jesus founded the church before there was
a felt need for it.

On the other hand, many find the church from
outside. It is thrust into their path. I am one of those
whose early home was not Christian; ethical and moral,
yes, but not "officially" Christian. Someone was out
there ahead to bring me in, and eventually the family
also came in.

Is this not the picture of God that is revealed

throughout the Bible? Here is the tremendous affirmation of our Christian life and strategy.

It means that when we are about God's business we don't have to try and drag God along with us. We are in it in the first place because God has drawn us there. Elijah was in that cave because he had done what God told him to do. This means that we have nothing to fear with regard to hindrances that may impede our path. If God is as the psalmist declared He is, and as God told Elijah, we will find Him already dealing with the obstacles. Elisha was out there, and so were 7,000 others.

For example, look at that little group of women who wanted to do a last service for the Master. Jesus had been crucified and buried. So they started out early one morning to anoint the dead body with the appropriate burial spices. Then, a startling act, the tomb was sealed with a stone. Then the melancholy cry: "[The stone!] Who will roll away the stone?" (Mark 16:3). And if you've never heard an Arabic wail, you've never heard a cacophony. It goes on and on in that weird Oriental tonal quality.

But notice: they did not stop and hold an emergency prayer meeting. They went on! When they came to the tomb, they found the stone already rolled away. God surprised them in advance. He was there first! And the first message to them was: "He goeth before you into Galilee" (Matt. 28:7, KJV). Jesus had already used this sentence when He said to the disciples, "After I am risen again, I will go before you into Galilee" (Matt. 26:32, KJV).

And this He has been doing ever since, going before us into the common, everyday places of Galilee.

Ours is a day fearful for the future of the church, fearful for the future of the total Christian movement. The rapid rise of communism in the past seven decades is one major cause of that fear. The resurgence of ancient religions such as Buddhism, Hinduism, and Islam —even in the United States—adds to that fear. The increasing secular materialism in our own country causes a dread. Crime statistics about murder, rape, and drugs indicate that ethical Christian living is on the wane. Not only this, but on the local church level there is cause for concern. Our own church has its share of spiritual apathy, as do other churches. Despite our Southern Baptist enthusiasm, there is considerable disinterest. Other Christian groups face the same general malaise. The cause of Christ is not as bright as we would like. We do wonder what will happen.

God has not left us alone. God is already out there ahead of us. The Holy Spirit is at work, as the wind blowing, though we do not see Him.

When John F. Kennedy was president of the United States he came up with a magnificent idea called the Peace Corps. In 1961 Congress made it official. It was an altruistic dream, and American youth responded. My soul, how they responded!

We should not have been surprised. Before the Peace Corps the Baptist Student Union had been sending students to serve as summer missionaries. Later our Foreign Mission Board created a means for two years of service called Journeymen. From 1965 through 1983 there have been 1,542 Journeymen, and 137 have become career missionaries—modern Elishas.[1] Then the Home Mission Board developed the US-2 program for two years of service in America. From 1965 through 1983 there have been 478 US-2ers, and sixty-five have become career missionaries: twenty-three with the Foreign Mission Board, forty-two with the Home Mission Board[2]—more modern Elishas. Then we went beyond that to make it possible for adults to serve for shorter periods, from one week to one year. My wife, Gladys, and I served for a summer in Bangkok, Thailand. We call that Bold Mission Thrust. And people have responded—even more modern Elishas out there waiting.

Let us therefore ask: "What does it mean to follow God out into this late twentieth century toward Damascus or Galilee?"

To follow brings us into sharp focus with the forces of evil. There is always a modern counterpart of Jezebel. The easy, surface peace of life is broken up into danger and difficulty. To follow demands an erect ethical posture, much harder to maintain than to sink back into a careless, depressed moral slump in a cave or cloister, or take our ease in unconcerned lounging in a comfortable "Zion."

To follow means the choice of intangibles: faith, hope, and love instead of prestige, power, and comfort.

To follow puts us out of step with the passing parade. Jesus is an irregular. If we try to follow Him we get out of step with the crowd. In the racial crises of the 1960s a prominent preacher said: "Jesus was a middle-of-the-roader." To which Dr. Frank Stagg replied: "Yes, Jesus was in the middle of the road. The thing is, Jesus was going in one direction, while everyone else was going the opposite way."

If there are Jezebels still among us, Elijahs are with

us, too, feeling depressed and alone. And God is still here as well.

At the Baptist World Alliance meeting in Miami, Florida, in 1965, Dr. Ithel Jones of Wales related this incident:

> I began my ministry (1938) in Porthcawl, a pleasant Welsh seaside resort. . . . In those days I belonged to the West Wales Baptist Association. I remember the Association Assembly being held in Neath, one of the industrial towns of South Wales, at which one of our abler young ministers had been invited to deliver an address on "Youth and the Church." . . . The young man read a carefully prepared paper for which he had collected data and statistics from all over the place. . . . This was his considered conclusion:

> "If things go on for another five years as they have gone on during these last five years, there'll be no Baptist churches left in South Wales."

> He had proved his point mathematically and a gloom fell upon the Assembly. The moment the young man took his seat, the minister of the church where the Assembly was being held, a dynamic veteran with a loud voice, took the platform and without ceremony addressed the congregation:

> "Mr. President, in the year 1920 I was president of the Association and delivered my presidential address at Maesteg. You were so impressed with it that you published it in pamphlet form! I proved conclusively in that address that if things went on for another five years as they had during the previous five years there would be no Baptist churches left in South Wales. That, Mr. President, was in 1920 and here we are in 1938 saying the same thing. There's something wrong somewhere. I have pleasure in moving, Mr. President, that no man be allowed to ascend

our platform within the next twenty years and base the prospects of the Christian church upon statistics."

I don't remember whether anyone seconded. And it was probably a blow below the belt to that young man. . . . But I am absolutely certain that the veteran minister was right . . . the most significant fact about the church has eluded the fact that a risen Saviour who has broken the bonds of death is going on before and beckoning us onward.[3]

The church does belie all human evaluations, all human prognosis. G. K. Chesterton once observed that Christianity has many times gone to the dogs, but in each case it was the dog that died! The church has many times appeared to have dwindled to nothing and has come alive again because God was in advance, waiting with a surprise. Let us never count God out!

God goes ahead of us and waits with the blessings of His goodness!

9

God and the Acquisitive Instinct
1 Kings 21:1-29; Matthew 19:21

It is good to have money and what money can buy, but it is also good to check up once in awhile and make sure we have not lost what money cannot buy!

George Frederick Watts was a famous English portrait painter in the middle nineteenth century. Watts's purpose in his paintings was to express objectively certain great truths of life. One of Watts's masterpieces was a portrait of the man whom we call the rich young ruler.

Cynthia Pearl Maus interprets the painting by pointing out that the face of the man is entirely hidden, so it is not easy to judge the man's age, character, or intellect. We see a man with a bowed head, drooping shoulders, and dressed in silk sleeves and a velvet, fur-trimmed mantle. Rings on his fingers and a massive gold chain around his shoulders indicate his wealth. The artist entitled the picture *For He Had Great Possessions.* As one looks at the picture, a phrase of Dante comes to mind: "One who made through cowardice the great refusal."

That is, without the armor of riches he did not have the nerve to face life. He had become the slave, not the master of material possessions. Looking further at the picture, we see a large, grasping hand,

> The fingers spread like talons; somewhat relaxed, . . . for this one moment of vain regret; but presently they will come together like a vise never again to open except to grasp some new object of desire.[1]

"The love of money, failing as it does to appreciate the worth of personality, brings upon the soul that it owns the loss of its own personality. The man is swallowed up by his own greed. All that gives him distinctiveness as a soul, as a member of society, as God's image, dies out, and only the elemental function of grabbing remains. That is why Watts does not show the man's face.

"When the love of money takes possession of the soul, one by one the virtues leave and the vices arrive. First, the fountains of sympathy are stopped; then the pride of life looks out at the windows—then arises the will to dominate rather than to serve."[2]

If an artist were to paint King Ahab, the same characterization could be used. That picture could be entitled "When a Man Has Everything, What More Can He Want?" King Ahab had everything, but he wanted more. Here's the story in brief.

A man named Naboth had a small vineyard which he had inherited. This vineyard was near the king's palace. Ahab wanted to buy the property for a vegetable garden. Naboth refused to sell because it was a family inheritance to be passed on to his sons. Ahab began to pout. After all, a king should have anything he wanted. Who was this peasant to refuse the king? So, Ahab took to his bed, turned his face to the wall, and refused to eat. Just like a petulant child.

Queen Jezebel found him, learned the reason for his sulking, and decided to take matters into her own hands. Her question of "what to give a man who has everything for his birthday" was answered by her use of diplomatic skill and coldhearted cruelty. She trumped up a false charge that Naboth had cursed both God and Ahab and found two "paid informers" to give testimony. One questions Jezebel's sudden concern for God. Naboth was condemned, and executed, as were his sons. Ahab then grasped his vineyard, quit sulking, ate again, and was happy.

But ol' Elijah heard about what happened, hurried to the palace, confronted Ahab, and threatened him with the wrath of God. Where had Elijah been all this time? What had he been doing? And how was it that he always got in to see the king when he was considered an enemy by Jezebel and she had a "contract" out on his life?

The evil course of Ahab reached its nadir in the killing of Naboth in order to steal his vineyard. His petty greed, his pliability in the hands of Jezebel, and his complicity in the death of an innocent man constituted evil of the worst kind. Ahab had sold his soul for the price of his neighbor's vineyard. The man who had everything forgot the Tenth Commandment, which presumably he knew: "Thou shalt not covet thy neighbor's house, his wife [David skipped over that one], his servant, his livestock, or *anything* that is thy neighbor's" (Ex. 20:17, author).

When Ahab saw Elijah, he cried out: "Have you

found me, O my enemy?" (1 Kings 21:20). To a guilty conscience the prophet of God (preacher) always looks like an enemy.

Let's at least give Ahab credit for not being all bad. He did retain a bit of sense about right and wrong. He sensed his wrong, was stricken with remorse, repented, and humbled himself before God. There is nothing to indicate his repentance was not genuine.

> And when Ahab heard those words, he rent his clothes and put sackcloth upon his flesh, and fasted and lay in sackcloth, and went about dejectedly. And the word of the Lord came to Elijah the Tishbite saying, "Have you seen how Ahab humbled himself before me?" (vv. 27-29).

And the doom was postponed for a generation.

Most of us are neither Ahab nor the rich young ruler, but the same sin of avarice attacks us at other points. Not even the poor escape it. Those in poverty can easily be greedy.

We were born with an acquisitive instinct, with a consuming desire to accumulate and possess. We are never completely rid of it. Nor should we be. Out of it comes most of our progress—and most of our problems. Animals have this instinct. Ants and squirrels store up for winter, and dogs bury bones for the future. We extol this virtue in the story of the grasshopper and the ant. Our baby hands reach out for things before there is any instruction. Sociologists and historians indicate that most of the vast migrations and expansions were born out of this acquisitive instinct. In the best sense, men such as Columbus were lured on by the call of undiscovered lands, by the gleam of gold, spices, and silk—the romance of riches. Man has always been a restless wanderer looking for the pot of gold at the end of a far-distant rainbow. At the worst level, since the pharaohs, Alexander the Great, the Roman Empire, and today, other men and nations have wanted to accumulate territory to add to their empires.

I know a woman now in her late seventies. She is wealthy and a good steward of her wealth. She is the largest contributer to her church's budget. The tithe of some of her stock gives some $10,000 annually to our denomination's foreign missions offering. She would be called unselfish. But she has a quirky, acquisitive instinct. On a world tour, with all meals provided, she would squirrel away snacks served on the airlines—rolls, butter, cheese—and from the hotel dining rooms, just in case. There was nothing wrong with her doing that. It merely illustrates the instinct.

Jesus was aware of this instinct. He told stories about a pearl of great price which a man had to have, and about a treasure hidden in a field. Jesus preached more about money, man's relationship to his environment, and his stewardship than anything else.

Woven into our nature is the passion to possess, and this passion can become a tyrant. Ah, my soul! the crimes and sins that have been committed by men and nations in their quest for one more small vineyard.

Someone once asked a very wealthy man, "How much wealth does it take to satisfy a man?" He answered, "Just a little more." Sometimes the "little more" is not for more money, but simply the excitement of doing it. I had a friend in Baton Rouge forty years ago. He had money, scads of it. He was an excellent

steward of what he had. One day he confided in me:
"Avery, I have more money than I need, more than I
can ever spend. But I'm addicted to the excitement of
making it."

Desire for more remains limitless because we can
never catch up with our imagination. As soon as one
desire is achieved, imagination makes the mouth water
for "a little more." Our mind begins to minimize the
objection and creates excuses for having that little more.
Ahab didn't need Naboth's vineyard, but he wanted it.

Sugar Ray Leonard, the boxer, has everything. He
has plenty of money and has received the highest ac-
colades. Why should he risk permanent blindness for a
little more adulation to massage his ego?

I heard of a woman who was poor enough to live
in public housing. She purchased a piano which she
could neither pay for nor play—just to impress her
neighbors.

We find it easy to talk against selfishness, but we
all love it. We are born with it. As we grow up, we know
we ought to be unselfish. We admire unselfishness, yet
we love selfishness. I am selfish, and so are you, and it's
not all bad. Some unselfishness, some good, is often
done for our own pleasure or to assuage our guilt, and
that is, therefore, selfish.

Paul penned that "the love of money is the root of
all evils" (1 Tim. 6:10). Most preaching on that text has
been negative. And, seeing the evil side, we do well to
stress the negative. But all the preaching in the world
will never stop people from seeking possessions. We
may enact legislation to curb the impulse to grab more,
but we cannot take away the impulse without removing

something natural. In our negative counsel there is a note of unreality. It does not face up to human nature. I read an amusing cartoon which illustrates. A man was pictured standing in a shower of money—ten, twenty, fifty dollar bills falling all around him. The caption read: "The root of evil and how to get more of it." Instead of trying to tear out the roots, why not try to cultivate the root in order to produce a better tree?

At first glance, Jesus seems to renounce the accumulation of wealth, restrain the passion to possess, or reduce desire to the level of bare existence. We are led to believe that He lived in poverty. I rather believe that this has been somewhat romanticized. Let's remember that the economic world of the first century was vastly different from ours. Jesus did work as a carpenter. He voiced no objections when wealthy friends supported Him and His ministry. The twelve were successful businessmen.[3] If some of us do not accumulate a few possessions, who will pay for the upkeep of those who do not?

I think it a mistake for us to take what Jesus said to that young man, "Go, sell what you possess and give to the poor," as being intended for everyone. Jesus never offered a patent medicine; He always gave a personal prescription. He prescribed what He did to that young man because his acquisitive instinct was standing between him and his desire for something more valuable, something he wanted even more—eternal life.

King Ahab was not censured for his possessions. Possessions went with the territory of being king. When he coveted one man's small vineyard, and Jezebel's deceit defrauded the man and led to his murder, so that Ahab could have one more possession, Elijah stepped in to pronounce God's rebuke. The prophet Nathan did not censure King David for his adulterous affair with Bathsheba so much as he did for David's taking "a poor man's lamb" instead of a lamb from his own flock. In fact, Nathan had God list all that had been given to David and then say, "if this were too little, I would add to you as much more" (2 Sam. 12:8).

In Ahab, David, and that young man we view men who seemingly had everything. Still, each was hungry for something more. Ahab wanted another vineyard. David wanted another woman. That young man was more sensitive in asking, "What do I lack? What can I do?"

The story of the rich young ruler is not to be applied as a moral for every situation. Jesus did not treat all rich men as He did this one. Jesus had many rich friends of whom He never made such a demand. Jesus gave no instructions to Zacchaeus. Zacchaeus himself volunteered: "... the half of my goods I give to the poor; and *if* I have defrauded anyone of anything, I restore it fourfold" (Luke 19:8, author's italics).

Jesus' suggestion was to this one man in this one situation, but the principle holds. Life is an unending exchange of things we can't keep for things we can't lose, things money cannot buy. The willingness to make the exchange is the indication of our sense of values.

Herein is the lesson about life's real meaning. It is what the New Testament calls *stewardship*. That is, the means by which money is transmuted into people and material possessions are exchanged for the riches of mind and spirit. That is what possessions are for. Money is not sinful. It is a part of us, an almost almighty something we plunk down on the counter of life and say, "Give me *that* for this." Said Jesus: "Follow me, and you shall have treasure worth having" (Author's words).

For me, this means a *responsible exchange.* The first responsibility is to God. And, for me, that is my tithe. It can be no less, and that goes to my church. The second responsibility is to my family. If I do not take care of them I am derelict. I also view the church as a family. If the church does not take care of its family, it too is derelict. The third responsibility is to other areas of need: missions, hunger, medical research, schools, whatever. And mine may not be yours. Whichever course we take it must be more than talk. I become weary, yes irritated, with those who tell me what I ought to be doing, and then do nothing themselves. This irritation begins with our president and continues to some fellow church members.

Now, let me try and put this together so that the Ahabs, rich young rulers, and all of us who have this acquisitive instinct may find a way out.

I began by noting that everyone has the acquisitive instinct. There is something else we all have—*self-regard.* The desire to amount to something is the very stuff out of which a worthwhile life is made. Saul of Tarsus, before he became a follower of the Man of Nazareth, was a forceful, assertive man, set on being somebody. After the "Damascus Road" experience he was no less so, despite his own self put-downs. But the redirection of this strong propulsion made his conversion one of the most notable events in history. Without the high use of this primary motivation, achievement in any realm is impossible. Some try to inhibit the desire by praying, "Oh, to be nothing, nothing!" And unfortunately for themselves and the others the prayer is answered.

Self-regard is not to be despised or suppressed. It is to be educated, directed, and used. At no point have conventional moralists done people more harm and disservice than in their disparagement of self-love. They sometimes wield the word *selfishness* as a bludgeon, cracking down on all forms of self-consideration until sensitive folk are convinced that whatever is to one's own advantage is wrong. Such unhealthy dishonoring of one of our most basic emotional instincts is both false to facts and dangerous to personal and social welfare.

Shakespeare's sound sense cannot be denied: "Self-love, my liege, is not so vile a sin as self-neglecting." Jesus expressed it better in His summary: "Love your neighbor as you love yourself."

Start with the love of self, take its measure, give full scope to its meaning at its best, then love your neighbor in the same manner. What we call "The Golden Rule" is impossible unless we begin with self-consideration and then extend that same consideration to everyone else.

When it is proposed that we cease caring for ourselves and care only for others, when self-regard and altruism are set against each other as being mutually exclusive, we are faced with a solution both psychologically impossible and ethically false. We cannot stop caring for ourselves, nor should we. We ought not to stop caring for ourselves. Our business is to care so much for ourselves that *I* tackles *me*, determined to make out of me something worthwhile. That is life's, a Christian's, primary demand. If we fail at that, we fail in everything. Nothing we can do for others matters except as we are of such an inherent quality that what we do is worthwhile. Unless we know how to love ourselves rightfully, we have neither the criterion nor the means of loving a neighbor or of doing anything for that neighbor.

Ah, Ahab, and you, young man, if you could have learned this lesson. If we, your successors, could even now grasp its significance, we would learn to check up once in awhile and make sure we have not lost that which money cannot buy.

10

God's Assurance that the Search Is Worthwhile

We began our excursion into the life of Elijah with our own personal search for God, saying: "O that I knew where I might find him." And we received the answer: "If with all your hearts ye truly seek Me, ye shall ever surely find Me."

During the journey we have faced trouble, seen victory, learned that evil never takes defeat lying down, that doing what we think is the will of God does not give us immunity from problems; stared at despondency, found that we are never alone, for God always leaves a remnant, all with this God whom we have sought, found, affirmed, and followed. Is it all worthwhile? And the answer to that is: "The glory of the Lord ever shall reward you. O Lord, our Creator, how excellent is Thy name in all the nations."

Some years ago four men spent their vacation together in Maine with an old fisherman as their guide. One man was a preacher, another a research physician, the third a geologist, and the other an astronomer. It was the summer when William Jennings Bryan was making his last attempt at the presidency, and rock-ribbed Republican Maine was worried. At night the men talked about the ages of the rocks, the theory of evolution, the immeasurable distance of the stars, and of God the Creator. The old fisherman listened. He'd never heard talk like that. Finally, his taciturnity broke down, and the questions poured from him like a flood: Were the rocks really so old? Did life evolve from the sea? Were the stars that far away? Was everything so vast and ancient? When at last he had grasped all of this in his mind, he heaved a sigh of relief and said: "Well, I guess it don't make a powerful lot of difference even if old William Jennings Bryan is elected."

With that, does it make a powerful lot of difference about Reagan, Bush, Hart, Jackson, Gorbachev, Assad, or Shamir, or even Ahab and Jezebel. But our reactions *do* make a difference. What life in the long run does to us depends upon what life finds in us now. There, in one sentence, is one of the most elemental and determining facts of human experience.

For example, two men go to the French Quarter in New Orleans. One is an investigative TV reporter, the other a dedicated Christian social worker. They see the same things, deal with the same people, and face the same circumstances. But how different are the results. One carries into that situation the instincts of a good reporter so that in "Walking on the Wild Side," he catches the filth from everything he sees and touches: strip joints, "head" shops, drug pushers, pimps, and prostitutes. He is dismayed at what he sees and finds, and his viewers are titillated and shake their heads, complaining: "Why doesn't somebody do something?" The other carries the spirit of a Savior so that he deepens his concern for people, has compassion for their weakness, shame for their sin, and a passion for their redemption. He *is doing* something. You see, it is not so much what life brings to us as it is what we bring to life in our spirit that makes the difference.

As a Christian, I leap from the Old Testament to the New Testament and hear Paul saying: "We know that to them that love God, who are called according to his purpose, all things work together for good" (Rom. 8:28, author).
If we omit the first part of that statement, the conclusion is incredible. All things of themselves do not work together for good, and we can't pretend that they do.

Into any situation, if we bring one set of interior attitudes, we will accrue the corresponding result, but if into that same situation we bring other attitudes we will come out somewhere else. What happens to us from outside of us does not determine the consequences. What happens to us from within pulls our trigger and explodes us. The consequences depend upon what is in us to explode. Putting this together, then:

> If with all your hearts ye truly seek me, ye shall ever surely find me, and when you do find me, everything isn't going to be easy, but it will all work out to your best interest. And you can count on that!

In this truth is an answer to the question: Is life worth living? How can one answer that in general? For multitudes of people, life clearly seems not worth living. Life may be worth living for the prosperous, the fortunate, who by heritage or achievement have been given the world's cushioned seats. But the ill-being, the baffled, hunger-stricken, cruelly handicapped, whipped and beaten men, women, and children, millions of them, life is not worth living. That is from our point of view, and perhaps from theirs.

To draw a line through humankind with good fortune on one side and ill fortune on the other, and simply say that only those on the good fortune side find life worth living, is to be mistaken. Some on each side will find life good or bad, or a mixture. Life itself has an appalling impartiality. Koheleth wrote: "All things come alike to all: there is one event to the righteous and to the wicked" (Eccl. 9:2, KJV).

Birth and death, joy and sorrow, health and sickness, love and loss, success and failure, happiness and tragedy, impartiality. "This world is not run right," we complain. When a hurricane wrecks a community, churches and schools fare no better than brothels or casinos. "And that's not fair!" we cry.

What makes the difference is the reaction.

I couldn't look over my congregations, as I did for these years, without pondering this matter. Today is unique. We never will all be together in this same situation again. When we go from here today we shall scatter, never to return exactly like this again—even if we all live and could assemble in this exact configuration. Ask what will happen to us and the answer is easy: life and death, joy and sorrow, success and failure, all kinds of things. What all these things do to us will depend upon what they find in us. But we shall never again be exactly the same.

Five hundred years after Elijah, the prophet Malachi wrote: "Behold, I will send you Elijah the prophet

before the great and terrible day of the Lord comes"
(Mal. 4:5).

Not really Elijah, no more than some thought of
Jesus as Elijah, or that Elijah is really expected to show
up at a Passover. Malachi was creating a link between
the generations. This is not easy, for the link often wears
thin and breaks. We say: "History repeats itself. We
learn nothing from history. We repeat the same mis-
takes. The more things change, the more they remain
the same."

There needs to be, ought to be, and must be some
continuity. But each generation ought to seek its own
direction and achieve its independence. Otherwise there
is no progress-development in history. The break with
the past must not and need not be complete or final. It
should always be a prelude to something more mature
and better. But there is an unbroken continuity in our
religious faith, our search for God. Successive generations share the Old Testament, the New Testament, and
Christian history.

If we watch too much TV news or read the newspapers too assiduously, our horizons become narrowly
limited to this world. That's where the continuity of our
faith comes in. There is a need for us to lift our eyes to
broader vistas. And that's one reason why we have been
looking at the Elijah saga and reading Mendelssohn's
mighty lyrics, to find meaning for ourselves in Elijah's
search for God.

His finding something that needed to be done, and
doing it, his conflict with Ahab, Jezebel, and the priests
of Baal, his despondency and cure.

Now we are coming to the conclusion. Seeing Elijah and learning from him, we can have our horizons lifted and broadened. To do that, let's look beyond him and see some other links: Isaiah 40:3-5 and Mark 1:2-4.

Each speaks of a troubled time, as troubled as Elijah faced, or what we face. Isaiah wrote during the Babylonian exile; Mark when Rome ruled Jerusalem and the known world. Today how unimportant are Baal and Babylon and the Roman Empire. But here we are reading, and finding inspiration, comfort, and challenge from these records of historic fact.

Almost everywhere these days one would listen eagerly to a voice that would tell us how to cope with the Middle East, smash the Soviets, brush off those pesky Cubans, or how to cure poverty and end injustice and oppression. As a Christian minister, concerned about all of this, I must appeal to you to be aware of a different kind of message with some answers to all of that, but one which has far greater significance in the end. And it is the same old message linking the present to the past:

> Behold, God sent Elijah.
> O come everyone that thirsteth,
> Come unto him.
> O hear, and your souls shall live forever
> And then, shall your light break forth
> And the glory of the Lord shall forever reward you.
> Lord our Creator, how excellent is Thy name in all the nations.
> Thou fillest heaven with Thy glory.

There are three truths about God which we need to remember:

1. God is greater than this world.
2. God works through this world.
3. God suffers with this world.

It is not easy to find an illustration, for the nature of God is so majestic that when we emphasize one aspect we neglect another; or like a many-faceted diamond which needs to be seen at all angles in pure light for us to be aware of its full beauty. Maybe it will help us to think of God in terms of our hands.

We are greater than our hands, transcendent above them, and would exist if we lost them. So is God in relation to His world.

We use our hands, work with them, express ourselves with them. So does God in relation to His world.

We feel by means of our hands, are sensitive to anything that wounds them, and suffer when they are injured. So is God in relation to His world of people.

If we are ever tempted to think that God is incapable of managing His world, that He has let it fall into a hopeless mess, and perhaps if we were in charge we could do a better job, think of a tiny spider crawling up the walls toward the steeple of a church. Perhaps his spidery mind is beset with terrific anxiety because he has somehow to negotiate one of the tiny crevices in the mortar between the brick. If he had sufficient thinking apparatus, which he doesn't, his anxiety and sense of insecurity would be increased a thousandfold. What possible picture could he have of a single brick, far less the building itself, and still less the purpose for which the building was built and exists? What possible clue could that spider have of the spiritual energies which have been sent out into the entire world from this building during its history? Could that spider have any idea at all about the life of this city?

It is not an exaggeration to comment that, in relation to the universe, we are like that spider. We know a little bit about our immediate haunts and the things that happen around us. But we know relatively little about our own planet. What is its purpose or what is God's purpose in this vast universe? We can only guess. But the remarkable fact is that such insignificant creatures as ourselves should have even a hint to enable us to guess.[1]

God must not, cannot, do for us what we can do for ourselves. But He works with us. In all things, *God works!* Behind all human enterprise something is given and something is demanded. Take any discovery: something to be discovered, and the brain to discover it, and the skill to make use of it. But something is demanded—the energy, devotion, wisdom, and patience to use it. Take a surgical instrument. God put iron in the hills. That is a given. But man had to find it, make steel from it, adapt and fashion the scalpel, and then someone must have the skill to use it. "Without God, we cannot; without us, God will not."

To have prevented the situation in Israel caused by Ahab and Jezebel, or to prevent the current world situation, God would have to rob us of the richest treasure we have hidden in us—*our free will!* Those who pray for God to stop the power of a dictator—a Castro or a Khomeini—are perhaps praying that God would become one himself.

In composing his oratorio, Mendelssohn used more of the Bible than the Elijah saga recorded in 1

Kings. In this section he turned to Isaiah to show the worthwhileness of God's covenant with Israel. The Babylonian exiles are to return. The covenant God made with Abraham, Moses, and Elijah will be kept. A new exodus, reminiscent of the event with which Israel's history began, will occur. The gift of the covenant is symbolized by freely given food and drink—manna in the wilderness, ravens, and a widow for Elijah.

In the Middle East water was and is a highly prized possession. It was bought and sold on the streets, as it is today in Cairo or old Jerusalem. So Isaiah took the cry of the water seller, "Ho, everyone who thirsts," and added ". . . [even] he who has no money" (Isa. 55:1). God's grace is utterly free. To those who accept God's grace the gift of new life is assured. It is an everlasting covenant.

Leslie Weatherhead stated that in Isaiah's day if a man became insolvent, the list of all his liabilities was written on a parchment and nailed up, with a nail at the top and another at the bottom, in some public place. If a rich friend saw this humiliating document he would sometimes take out the bottom nail, double the parchment in two, write his name across the folded document, and drive the nail in again at the top, securing the parchment in this folded form. His signature meant that he would be responsible for his friend's debts.[2]

History tells us that there was a book which recorded the taxes to be exacted from each town and village in France. The page headed *Domrey* was said to be doubled back, and across the folded portion one found the words written: "Free for the Maid's sake."

This is what Isaiah was describing when he called out:

> Comfort ye, comfort ye my people, saith your God. Speak ye comfortably to Jerusalem, and cry unto her, that her warfare is accomplished, that her iniquity is pardoned: for she hath received of the Lord's hands double for all her sins (Isa. 40:1-2, KJV).

Now, while I do a personal recapitulation, seeing something of myself in the Elijah story, put yourself in the picture and see where you are.

I have searched for God, and found Him, not all of Him, not as much as a Francis of Assisi or a Billy Graham, but enough of God to give me confidence and desire to search for more of Him and enough to believe I'm headed in the right direction.

I've tried to find and do God's will, not always certain of what it is, and sometimes mistakenly going off on my own, with good intentions. Occasionally, there have been disappointment, some frustration, and a bit of discouragement, but never the feeling that God has let me down.

I've never had a dramatic Mount Carmel conflict although there have been some skirmishes, some of them victorious.

I've never been in the despond of a wilderness cave, but I have been to the edges, and sometimes gone a bit farther in.

After these nearly fifty years of preaching, I have an inner assurance that life has been worthwhile, and there is more to come.

On a seacoast a boy once asked an old sailor,

"What is the wind?" After a long pause the old man answered: "I don't know. I can't tell you. But I know how to hoist a sail!"

There are endless unanswered questions about the wind, but still the wind is real. Hoist your sail and see! There are endless unanswered questions about God, but God is real! Search, find, see, and hoist the sail of your life with Him! "And the glory of the Lord shall ever reward you. O Lord, our Creator, How excellent is Thy name in all the nations. Amen."

Heavenly Father, would that we could more fully appreciate the excellency of Your name so that our trust in You would be more like that of Elijah. We are inspired by such men. Something stirs inside us, and we want to be that way, and sometimes we are. The world needs its Elijahs, but it needs the others of us as well. We can't all be the same, for we're not all alike in ability or temperament or faith. We are searching for You. We would now realize the fulfillment of that search by an acceptance of Jesus Christ, for Your fullness is to be found in Him.

Yes, Heavenly Father, the search for You is worthwhile, even when we don't find all that we're looking for. To find even a small part of the Eternal God and relate our life to that is our greatest joy. We know more about You than Elijah did because we have had Jesus Christ. As we take leave of the prophet, we would keep something of him with us so we would hoist our sails to face life in the confidence that You are with us.

NOTES

Chapter 1

1. James Weldon Johnson, *God's Trombones* (New York: Viking Press, 1927).

Chapter 2

1. Davie Napier, *Word of God, Word of Earth* (Philadelphia: United Church Press, 1976).

Chapter 4

1. Chaim Potok, *The Book of Lights* (New York: Alfred A. Knopf Press, 1981), p. 229.
2. Quoted by Robert Penn Warren, *Chief Joseph of the Nez Perce* (New York: Random House, 1982), p. 4.
3. Mead, *Encyclopedia of Religious Quotations.*
4. Napier, Ibid., p. 46.

Chapter 5

1. Wilmer C. Fields in *The Saturday Evening Post,* April 1983, p. 71.

Chapter 6

1. Cf. Napier, p. 58.
2. Napier, p. 60.
3. Napier, p. 65.

Chapter 7

1. "Foreign Missions in Battle Array" from *The Collected Poems* of Vachel Lindsay (New York: Macmillan, 1925).
2. Reprinted with permission of Macmillan Publishing Co., Inc. from J. B. Phillips: *The New Testament in Modern English,* Revised Edition. © J. B. Phillips 1958, 1960, 1972.
3. William Barclay, *The Daily Bible Study Series,* Revised Edition, "The Gospel of John, Vol. 1" (Philadelphia: The Westminster Press, 1975), pp. 42-43.

Chapter 8

1. Letter from Mrs. Barbara Kuntze, News and Information Department, Foreign Mission Board of the Southern Baptist Convention, Richmond, Virginia, dated April 5, 1984.
2. Letter from Ms. Mary D. Carver, Missions Ministries Division, Home Mission Board of the Southern Baptist Convention, Atlanta, Georgia, dated May 22, 1984.
3. Cf. *Baptist World Alliance Proceedings,* 1965.

Chapter 9

1. Cynthia Pearl Maus, *Christ and the Fine Arts* (New York: Harper & Brothers, 1959), p. 292.
2. Albert Edward Bailey quoted in Maus, Ibid., pp. 293-294.
3. See my book, *The Glorious Company* (Nashville: Broadman Press, 1986).

Chapter 10

1. Leslie D. Weatherhead, *This Is the Victory* (Nashville: Abingdon-Cokesbury Press, 1941), p. 72.
2. Ibid.

Passages from Mendelssohn's *Elijah*

Relating to Chapter 1. A Personal Search for God

Recitative—Obadiah

Ye people, rend your hearts, and not your garments, for your transgressions the prophet Elijah hath sealed the heavens through the word of God. I therefore say to ye, Forsake your idols, return to God; for He is slow to anger, and merciful, and kind, and gracious, and repenteth Him of the evil (Joel 2:12-13).

Air—Tenor

If with all your hearts ye truly seek Me, ye shall ever surely find Me. Thus saith our God. Oh! that I knew where I might find Him, that I might even come before His presence (Deut. 4:29; Job 23:3).

Chorus—The People

Yet doth the Lord see it not; He mocketh at us; His curse hath fallen down upon us; His wrath will pursue us till He destroy us! For He, the Lord our God, He is a jealous God; and He visiteth all the fathers' sins on the children to the third and the fourth generation of them that hate Him. His mercies on thousands fall— fall on all them that love Him and keep His commandments! (Deut. 28:22; Ex. 20:5-6).

Recitative—An Angel (Contralto)

Elijah! get thee hence, Elijah; depart and turn eastward; thither hide thee by Cherith's brook. There shalt thou drink its waters; and the Lord thy God hath commanded the ravens to feed thee there; so do according unto His word (1 Kings 17:3-4).

Semi-chorus—Angels

For He shall give His angels charge over thee; that they shall protect thee in all ways thou goest; that their hands shall uphold and guide thee, lest thou dash thy foot against a stone (Ps. 91:11-12).

Relating to Chapter 2. In Finding and Following God, What Do We Get?

Recitative—An Angel (Contralto)

Now Cherith's brook is dried up, Elijah, arise and depart, and get thee to Zarepath; thither abide; for the Lord hath commanded a widow woman there to sustain thee. And the barrel of meal shall not waste, neither shall the cruse of oil fail, until the day that the Lord sendeth rain upon the earth (1 Kings 17:7,9,14).

Recitative—Air, and Duet

—The Widow (Soprano)

What have I to do with thee, O man of God? art thou come to me to call my sin unto remembrance? to slay my son art thou come thither? Help me, man of God, my son is sick! and his sickness is so sore, that there is no breath left in him! I go mourning all the day long, I lie down and weep at night! See mine affliction. Be thou the orphan's helper! Help my son! There is no breath left in him!

—Elijah

Give me thy son. Turn unto her, O Lord my God, O Turn in mercy; in mercy help this widow's son! For Thou art gracious, and full of compassion, and plenteous in mercy and truth. Lord, my God, let the spirit of this child return, that he may again live!

—The Widow

Wilt thou show wonders to the dead? There is no breath in him!

—Elijah

Lord, my God, let the spirit of this child return, that he may again live!

—The Widow

The Lord hath heard thy prayer, the soul of my son reviveth!

—Elijah

Now behold, thy son liveth.

—The Widow

Now by this I know that thou art a man of God, and that His word in thy mouth is the truth. What shall I render to the Lord for all His benefits to me?

—Both

Thou shalt love the Lord thy God, love Him with all thine heart, and with all thy soul, and with all thy might. O blessed are they who fear Him (1 Kings 17:19,21-24; Job 10:15; Ps. 38:6, 6:6, 10:14, 86:15-16, 88:10, 116:12; Deut. 6:5; Ps. 128:1).

Chorus

Blessed are the men who fear Him; they ever walk in the ways of peace. Through darkness riseth light to the upright. He is gracious, compassionate; He is righteous (Ps. 128:1, 112:1,4).

Relating to Chapters 3. and 4. Affirming Who Is to Be God (I & II) and Chapter 5. One of God's Little Clouds

Recitative and Air—Elijah

Draw near, all ye people; come to me! Lord God of Abraham, Isaac, and Israel; this day let it be known that Thou art God; and I am Thy servant! O show to all this people that I have done these things according to Thy word! O hear me, Lord, and answer me; and show this people that Thou art Lord God; and let their hearts again be turned! (1 Kings 18:30,36,37).

Chorus—Angels

Cast thy burden upon the Lord, and He shall sustain thee. He never will suffer the righteous to fall; He is at thy right hand. Thy mercy, Lord, is great; and far above the heavens. Let none be made ashamed that wait upon Thee (Ps. 55:22, 16:8, 108:4, 25:3).

Recitative with Chorus—Obadiah

O man of God, help thy people! Among the idols of the Gentiles, are there any that can command the rain, or cause the heavens to give their showers? The Lord our God alone can do these things.

—Elijah

O Lord, Thou hast overthrown Thine enemies and destroyed them. Look down on us from heaven, O Lord; regard the distress of Thy people; open the heavens and send us relief; help, help Thy servant now, O God!

—The People

Open the heavens and send us relief; help, help Thy servant now, O God!

—The Youth

There is nothing. The heavens are as brass, they are as brass above me.

—Elijah

When the heavens are closed up because they have sinned against Thee, yet if they pray and confess Thy Name, and turn from their sin when Thou didst afflict them; then hear from heaven, and forgive the sin! Help; send Thy servant help, O God!

—The People

Then hear from heaven, and forgive their sin! Help! send Thy servant help, O Lord!

—Elijah

Go up again, and still look toward the sea.

—The Youth

There is nothing. The earth is as iron under me!

—Elijah

Hearest thou no sound of rain?—seest thou nothing arise from the deep?

—The Youth

No; there is nothing.

—Elijah

Have respect to the prayer of Thy servant, O Lord, my God! Unto Thee I will cry, Lord, my rock; be not silent to me; and Thy great mercies remember, Lord!

—The Youth

Behold, a little cloud ariseth now from the waters; it is like a man's hand. The heavens are black with clouds and wind; the storm rusheth louder and louder!

—The People

Thanks be to God, for all His mercies!

—Elijah

Thanks be to God, for He is gracious, and His Mercy endureth for evermore.

—The People

Thanks be to God! He laveth the thirsty land! The waters gather, they rush along; they are lifting their voices! The stormy billows are high, their fury is mighty. But the Lord is above them, and Almighty! (Jer. 14:22; 2 Chron. 6:19,26-27; Deut. 28:23; Ps. 28:1, 106:1; 1 Kings 18:43-45; Ps. 93:3-4).

Relating to Chapter 6. When the Bottom Drops Out, God Confirms Himself

Air—Elijah

It is enough; O Lord, now take my life, for I am not better than my fathers! I desire to live no longer; now let me die, for my days are but vanity! I have been very jealous for the Lord God of Hosts! for the children of Israel have broken Thy covenant, and thrown down Thine altars, and slain all Thy prophets—slain them with the sword; and I, even I only, am left; and they seek my life to take it away (Job 7:16; 1 Kings 19:4,10).

Recitative—Tenor

See, now he sleepeth beneath a juniper tree in the wilderness; and there be angels of the Lord encamped round about all them that fear Him (1 Kings 19:5; Ps. 34:7)

Three-part Boys' Choir—The Angels

Lift thine eyes to the mountains, whence cometh help. Thy help cometh from the Lord, the Maker of heaven and earth. He hath said, thy foot shall not be moved; thy Keeper will never slumber. (Ps. 121:1-3).

Chorus—Angels

He, watching over Israel, slumbers not, nor sleeps. Shouldst thou, walking in grief, languish, He will quicken thee (Ps. 121:4, 138:7).

Recitative—The Angel (Contralto)

Arise, Elijah, for thou hast a long journey before thee. Forty days and forty nights shalt thou go to Horeb, the mount of God (1 Kings 19:7-8).

—Elijah

O Lord, I have laboured in vain; yea, I have spent my strength for nought! O that Thou wouldst rend the heavens, that Thou wouldst come down; that the mountains would flow down at Thy presence, to make Thy Name known to Thine adversaries, through the wonders of Thy works! O Lord, why hast Thou made them to err from

Thy ways, and hardened their hearts that they do not fear Thee?
O that I now might die! (Isa. 49:4, 64:1-2, 63:17; 1 Kings 19:4).

Air—The Angel (Contralto)
O rest in the Lord; wait patiently for Him, then He shall give thee
thy heart's desires. Commit thy way unto Him, and trust in Him,
and fret not thyself because of evil doers (Ps. 37:1,4-7).

Chorus
He that shall endure to the end, shall be saved (Matt. 24:13).

*Relating to Chapter 10. God's Assurance that the Search Is
Worthwhile*

Recitative—Soprano
Behold, God hath sent Elijah the prophet, before the coming of the
great and dreadful day of the Lord. Then he shall turn the heart
of the fathers to the children, and the heart of the children unto
their fathers; lest the Lord shall come and smite the earth with a
curse (Mal. 4:5-6).

Chorus
But the Lord, from the north hath raised one, who from the rising
of the sun shall call upon His Name and come upon princes.
Behold, my servant and mine elect, in Whom my soul delighteth!
On Him the spirit of God shall rest; the spirit of wisdom and
understanding, the spirit of might and of counsel, the spirit of
knowledge and of the fear of the Lord. Thus saith the Lord: "I have
raised one from the north, who from the rising, on My Name shall
call" (Isa. 41:25, 42:1, 11:2).

Quartet
O come everyone that thirsteth, O come to the waters; O come unto
Him. O hear, and your souls shall live for ever (Isa. 55:1-3).

Chorus
And then shall your light break forth as the light of the morning
breaketh; and your health shall speedily spring forth then; and the
glory of the Lord ever shall reward you. Lord, our Creator, how
excellent Thy Name is in all the nations! Thou fillest heaven with
Thy glory. Amen (Isa. 58:11; Ps. 8:1).